MINIMALIST SPACES

"When one sees the solidity of a mountain or the vastness of the sea, when one comes upon it suddenly, it has a powerful, monolithic presence. Everything, including one's own ego, is pushed aside, except the majesty of that mountain or that sea. Such a sight absorbs you completely – it is beauty itself. If you are fortunate enough, think of a building with the same all-consuming intensity – that building I call architecture; the others are nothing but structures."
Claudio Silvestrin

"The Minimum could be defined as the perfection an artifact achieves when it can no longer be improved by subtraction. This is the quality that an object has when every component, every detail, and every junction has been reduced or condensed to the essential. It results from the omission of the inessential." *John Pawson*

Publisher	Paco Asensio
Editor and text	Aurora Cuito
Translation	Harry Paul
Proofreading	Julie King
Art Director	Mireia Casanovas Soley
Layout	Emma Termes Parera
D.L.	B-5276/2000
Printed in Spain	Gráficas Apipe

2001 © Loft Publications S.L. and HBI, an imprint of HarperCollins Publishers

First published in 2001 by LOFT and HBI, an imprint of HarperCollins Publishers 10 East 53rd St. New York, NY 10022-5299

Distributed in the U.S. and Canada by Watson-Guptill Publications 770 Broadway New York, NY 10003-9595 Ph.: (800) 451-1741 or (732) 363-4511 in NJ, AK, HI Fax: (732) 363-0338

Distributed throughout the rest of the world by HarperCollins International 10 East 53rd St. New York, NY 10022-5299 Fax: (212) 207-7654

We have tried our best to contact all copyright holders. In individual cases where this has not been possible, we request copyright holders to get in touch with the publishing house.

If you would like to suggest projects for inclusion in our next volumes, please e-mail details to us at: loft@loftpublications.com

ÍNDEX

4 Introduction

6 Homes

8 Na Xemena House
Ramon Esteve
16 House 2/5
Shigeru Ban
24 White apartment
Frank Lupo & Daniel Rowen
32 Type/Variant House
Vicent James & Paul Yaggie
40 M House
Kazuyo Sejima & Ryue Nishizawa
46 B House
Claudio Silvestrin
50 Y House
Katsufumi Kubota
58 Minimalist apartment
John Pawson
64 House in Staufen
Morger & Degelo
72 Panoramic House
Aranda, Pigem & Vilalta

80 Offices and Public Buildings

82 Graf Offices
Baumschlager & Eberle
90 Bathing Pavilion
Aranda, Pigem & Vilalta
94 Ridaura's civic center
Aranda, Pigem & Vilalta
100 Law School
Aranda, Pigem & Vilalta
106 No Picnic Offices
Claesson Koivisto Rune Arkitektkontor

112 Osho International Offices
Daniel Rowen
118 Architecture studio
GCA Arquitectos Asociados
122 Information center
Simon Conder Associates
126 Crematorium in Berlin
Axel Shultes + Charlotte Frank
132 Bang & Olufsen Offices
KHR AS

140 Commercial Spaces

142 Antonio Pernas Boutique
Iago Seara
150 Wagamama Restaurant
David Chipperfield Architects
154 One Happy Cloud Restaurant
Claesson Koivisto Rune Arkitektkontor
160 Julie Sohn Boutique
Conrado Carrasco & Carlos Tejada
166 A jewelry shop in Munich
Landau & Kindelbacher
172 Jigsaw Boutique
John Pawson
180 MA Gallery
Hiroyuki Arima + Urban Fourth
186 Dolce & Gabbana Boutique
David Chipperfield Architects & P+ARCH
190 Principe Boutique
Antonio Citterio & Partners
194 Fausto Santini Boutique
Antonio Citterio & Partners
198 Louis Vuitton Boutiques
Peter Marino & Associates

Introduction

As architecture evolves, certain trends are repeated, but adapted to the times. After periods of great upheaval or excess, the architectural focus changes and, usually, there is a return to moderation. Ornamentation is forced aside and architects search for essential elements. The 20th Century, guided by the Modern Movement, experienced an identity crisis at the end of the sixties that led to the emergence of Minimalism and Pop Art. Later, in total opposition to Postmodernism and Deconstructionism, currents began to appear which rejected trivial formalization.

For the minimalists, it meant going back to the begin, order to reach the essence of architecture through the minimum of gestures. Minimalism is not only negation, subtraction, and purity: it involves the reduction of the creative process to the basic concepts of light, volume, and mass. This austere and simple formalization, which sometimes conceals complex technical construction, eliminates all superfluous elements and results in a clear, intense perception of the creations.

This book is a journey through minimalist architecture. It examines diverse projects which are grouped into three chapters: homes, offices and public buildings, and commercial spaces. However, the projects included in the book share the desire to create a particular architectural work which, to be understood, does not need to be accompanied by an explanation or a reflection on what was evoked or how it was accomplished. Rather, the aim is simply to observe the designs and the way they interact with their surroundings.

Homes

Na Xemena House

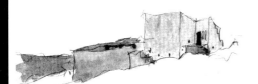

Na Xemena is located in northeastern Ibiza, a Mediterranean island which would be a prime location for any building. In this stark, rocky landscape by the sea, with cliffs jutting out into the Mediterranean, the architect establishes a balance and a dialogue between the terrain and the house. Equilibrium is architecture's most seductive and most extraordinary quality and the one that must endure.

The building's plans are fluid and natural. Although the design has a rational basis, the architect did not impose a rigid geometrical outline. The house can be continually expanded following the pattern of the original core. The rooms which make up the interior vary in size and shape, and are added onto the main structure along the rising ground.

The dwelling climbs the rocky base as a compact whole paralleling the contour of the cliff. From the outside, the arrangement of the terrace and swimming pool leads the eye to the emphatic shapes of the house. The entire complex strives to be a logical and unobtrusive extension of the landscape, in harmony with its surroundings.

The clean exterior walls are broken to capture light, following a natural order determined by the interior room arrangement, in which occupied space predominates over empty space. The exterior colors are from natural pigments: gray for the ground and terraces, derived indigo for the vertical surfaces.

Three large windows made from iroko wood frame views of the terraces and swimming pool. The pool seems to be a sheet of water blending with the sea. The interior walls, white and cobalt blue, illuminated by skylights, act as a unifying element throughout the house.

Architect:
    Ramon Esteve
Collaborators:
    Juan A. Ferrero,
    Antonio Calvo
Photographer:
    Ramon Esteve
Location:
    Ibiza, Spain
Completion date:
    1997
Floor space:
    3,340 square fee

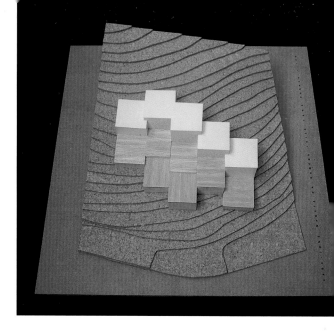

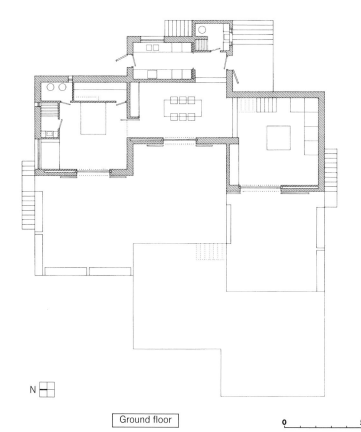

West elevation

South elevation

North elevation

0   5

East elevation

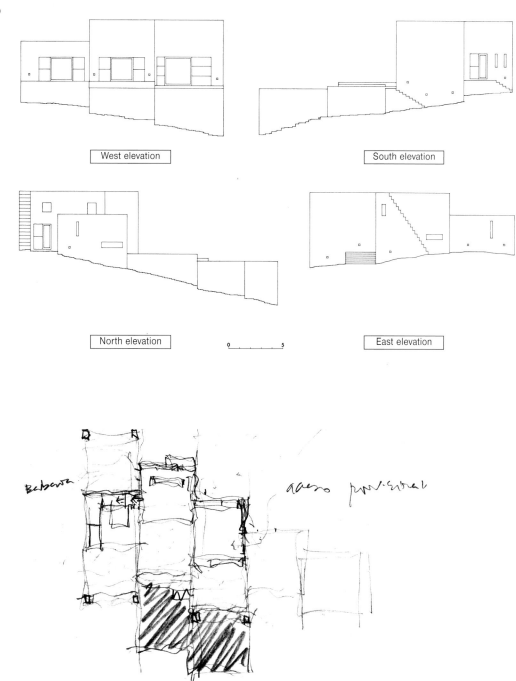

N

Ground floor

0   5

Right. The tables, benches and seats
in the living room and on the terrace.
Below. The outdoor stairs and
the magnificent views.

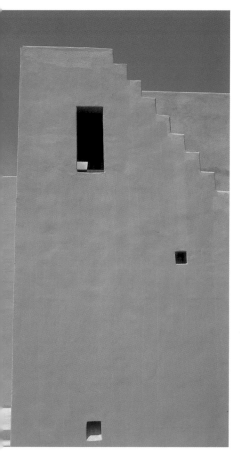

Next page. Different views of the living room.
Pages 14-15. The staircase in the interior is
one of the main design elements in the house.

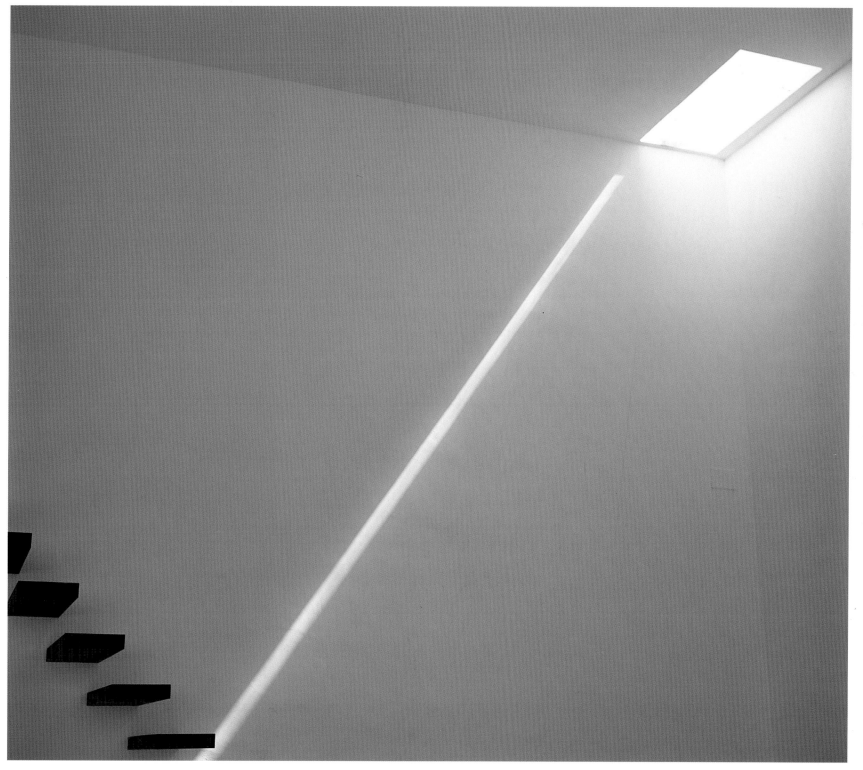

House 2/5

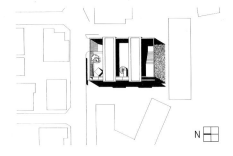

N

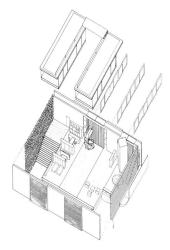

House 2/5 is part of a series of experimental structures based on the exploration of space and light and their interrelationships with the environment. Designed for intrepid clients, each prototype attempts to be the perfect dwelling in all facets of domestic life.

The building, located on the outskirts of the city, had as its principal objective isolation from the noise and pollution of the urban environment. To achieve this, the architect, Shigeru Ban, incorporated an alternative version of the traditional domestic patio. The total surface area was divided into five equal strips alternating interiors with gardens and terraces.

The home is bordered on the east and west by two-story concrete walls. On the north face, thick PVC netting secludes the residence. On the street front, a perforated, corrugated aluminum screen provides a view of the garage ramp. A separate door leads to a corridor that runs along one side of the house, connecting the succession of patios and living areas.

Ban integrated the patios with the interiors through sliding glass doors that open to form an enormous common area with a dense hedge as the back wall. Thanks to the way the glass walls and numerous interior screens are placed, the residence –living rooms, dining room, kitchen, and bedrooms– becomes the perfect stage for everyday home life.

The three patios can be protected from the elements by manually operated canopies.

Although the building is influenced by traditional Japanese architecture (the fluid interpretation of space, the austere materials, and the relationship with nature), the house responds imaginatively to the requirements of contemporary life.

Architect:
Shigeru Ban
Collaborators:
Hoshino Architect & Engineer
(structure), Matsumoto Corporation
(contractor)
Photographer:
Hiroyuki Hirai
Location:
Nishinomiya, Japan
Completion date:
1995
Floor space:
5,450 square feet

18

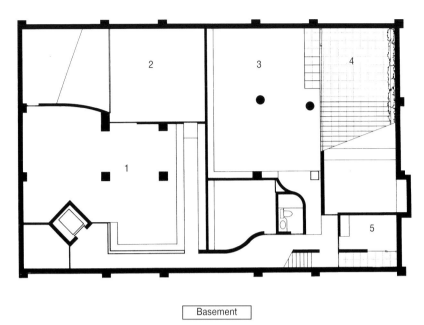

Basement

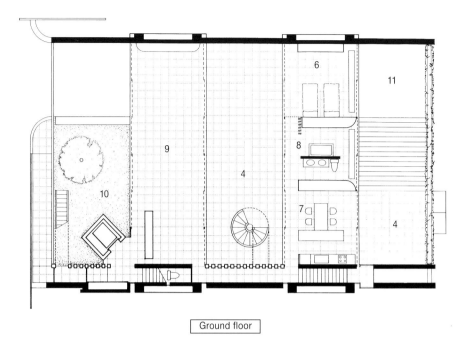

Ground floor

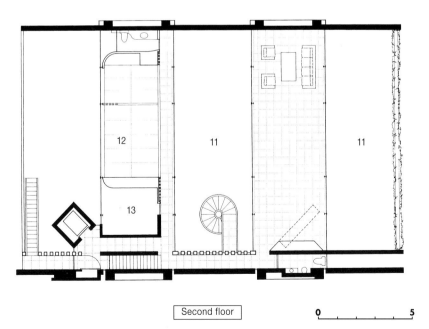

Second floor

1. Storage
2. Garage
3. Library
4. Terrace
5. Service room
6. Bedroom
7. Kitchen/dining room
8. Bathroom
9. Living room
10. Garden
11. Empty space
12. Tatami room
13. Children's rooms

0   5

Next page. View of the main façade.

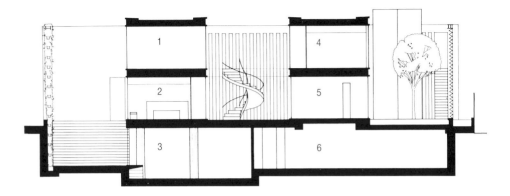

1. Living room
2. Bathroom
3. Library
4. Tatami room
5. Dining room
6. Storage

Section

View of the interior through the five strips.

Entry stairs to the ground floor of the house.

Next page. View of the interior patio and the roof. Different views of the interiors.

White Apartment

This project joined two traditional apartments located on Park Avenue (New York, USA) into one. The new interior space communicates the idea of abstraction, reinforced by the elimination of several windows and the use of translucent screens.

The notable absence of furniture was the client's idea.

He was drawn to the play of light against the diverse planes of the walls, floors and ceilings.

The wood floors are painted white, as are the walls and ceilings. The partition walls are slightly separated from the floors, so as not touch to them. This technique gives the sensation that the partition walls are not fixed and are able to move. The hallway doors extend from the floor to the ceiling and the rails that support them are built-in, so that only the plane of the door is visible. Screens made of translucent white fabric filter the space and isolate it visually from the exterior.

The supports and accessories that operate the screens are also invisible.

The minimalist aesthetic of the apartment creates a landscape of meditation that is radically different from the energies and influences of Manhattan.

The reductionist separation of this project gives the occupant a space in which to explore his feelings without interruption. This is a place to listen to light, to see silence, and to dream.

Architects:
Frank Lupo & Daniel Rowen

Collaborator:
FranK Lupo, Daniel Rowen, Jennifer Brayer, Celeste Umpierre & Ron Crawford (project team); Severud Associates (structural engineer); Ambrosio Depinto & Schmieder (mechanical engineer); John Deep Inc. (glass fabrication); Fisher Marantz Renfro Store (lighting consultant); C. Clark Construction Corporation (general contractor)

Photographer:
Michael Moran

Location:
New York City, USA

Completion date:
1995

Floor space:
1,600 square feet

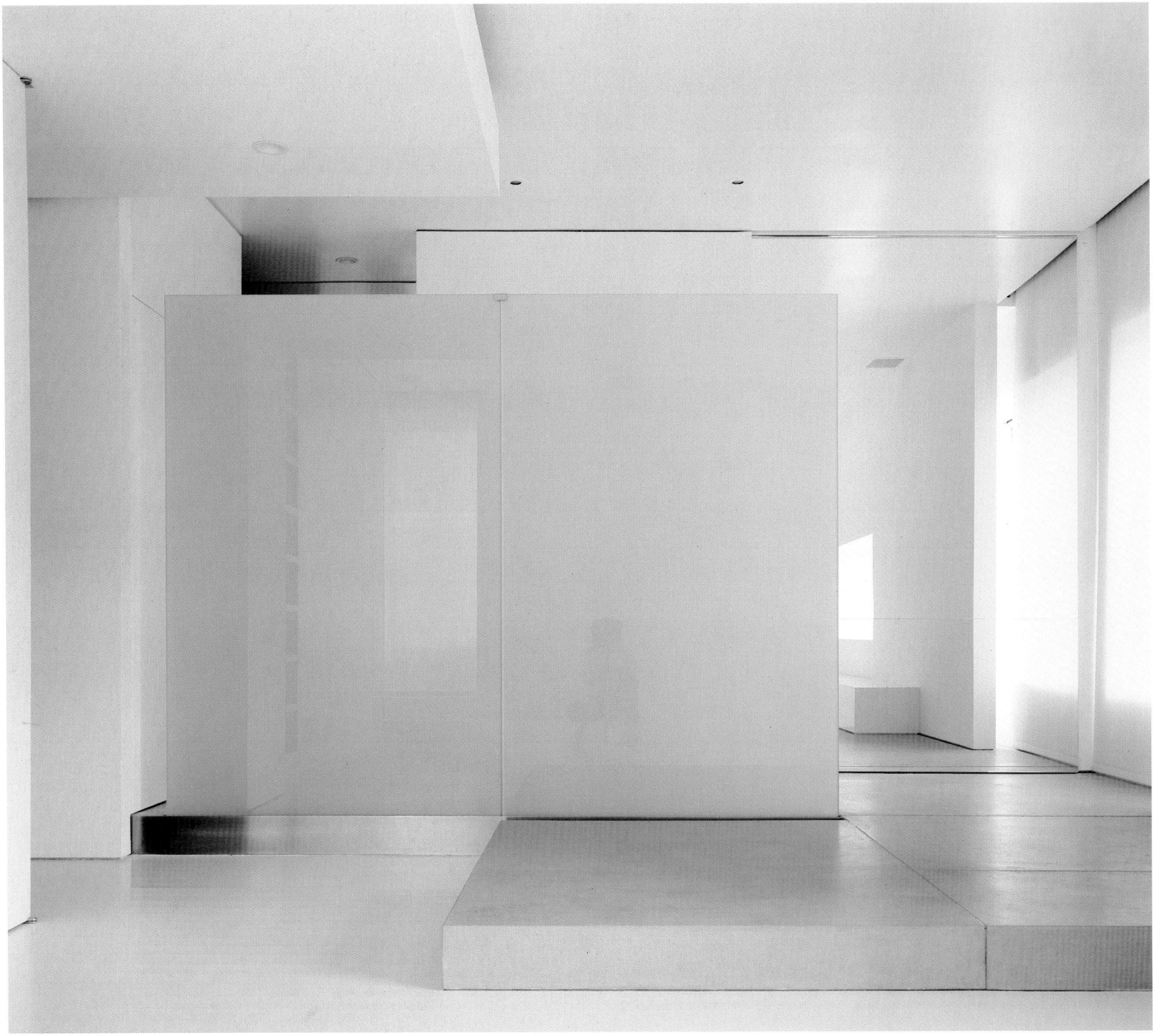

Previous page. Screens of translucent white isolate the space from the outside.

The diverse planes of the walls offer multiple views oh the interior spaces.

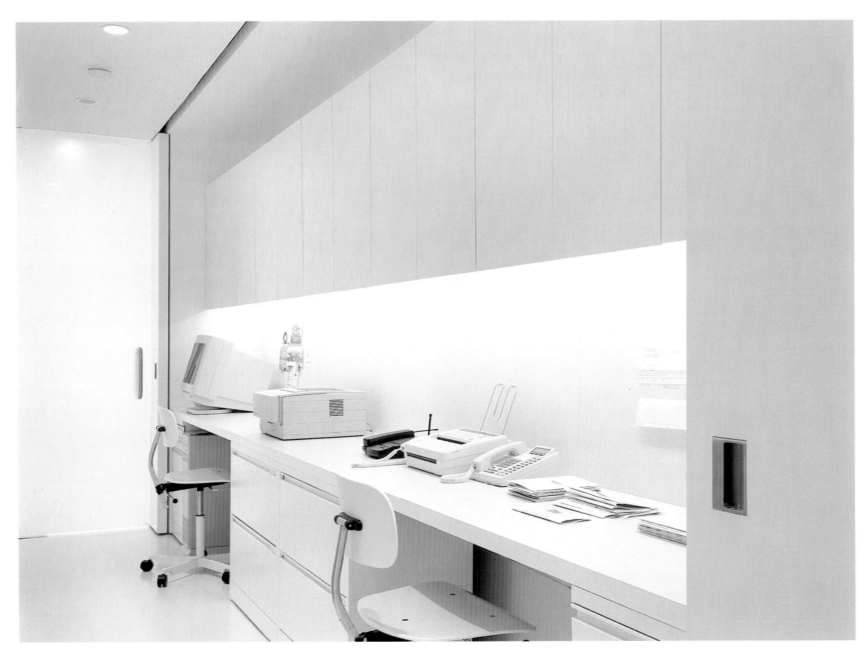

The client's office is also located in the dwelling. This work space follows the same design principles as the rest of the project.

Detail of the stainless steel bathroom sink.

Type/Variant House

The clients based this project on a concept that fascinated them, which they describe using the term "Type/Variant." This can be understood as taking one "type" of object and forming a collection of similar objects. A good example is a butterfly collection displayed in a glass box. The subtle differences among the butterflies create interesting relationships and, together, they have a strong aesthetic impact.

The architects incorporated the "Type/Variant" concept into the design of the project. In this case, the house is the composite of volumes which are variations on the theme of a box, with individual proportions, orientation, and natural light sources. When placed in an orthogonal composition, the wooden boxes create a house that responds to life's rhythms and patterns, with constantly changing views of the surroundings. Similarly, the turns and angles of the building's parts define various exterior spaces.

The composition is based on macles (twinned crystals) with parallelepipeds at different heights and various orientations. Group activities take place in the larger rooms and on outdoor terraces located in the central part of each structure. More private moments occur where the individual boxes meet, in the smaller, more enclosed areas.

The bedrooms, like the patios, are conceived as simple spaces that come to life with daily use and the cycle of the seasons. The exterior materials, especially the copper panels and bluish stone, are placed in a varied pattern which gives the walls rhythm and texture. The copper covering will not protect the faces from the weather and erosion. In fact, a key design element is that the house will evolve over time.

Architects:
    Vincent James & Paul Yaggie
Collaborators:
    Nancy Blanfard, Nathan Knuston,
    Andrew Dull, Steve Lazen, Krista
    Scheib, Julie Snow, Taavo Somer,
    Kate Wyberg (design team), Coen +
    Stumpf and Associates (landscaping),
    Yerigan Construction (contractor)
Photographer:
    Don F. Wong
Location:
    Northern Wisconsin, USA
Completion date:
    1996
Floor space:
    7,500 square feet

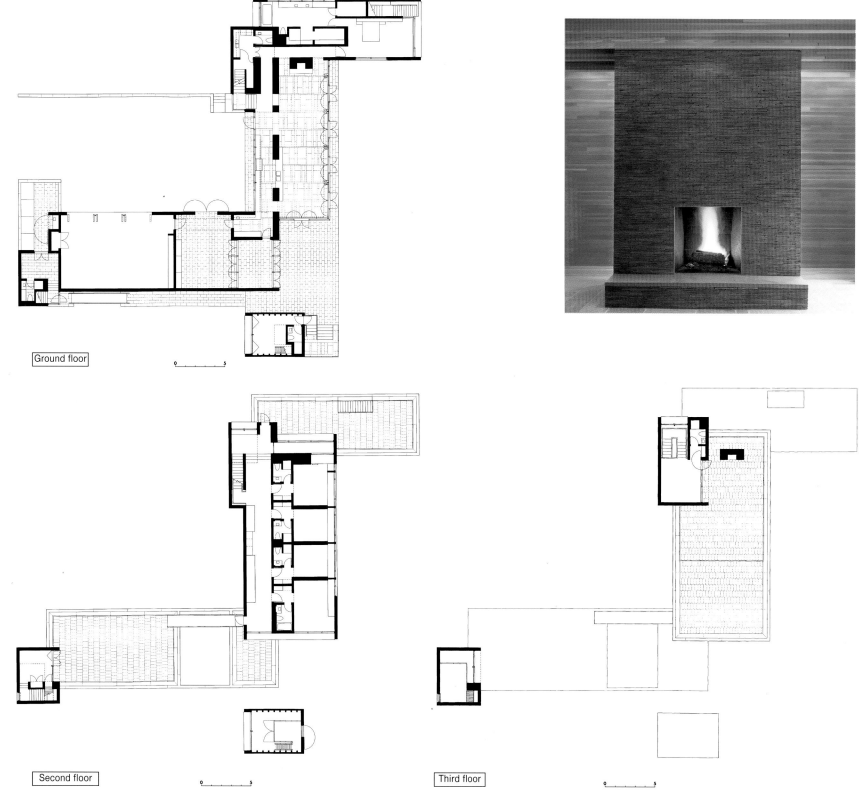

34

Ground floor

Second floor

Third floor

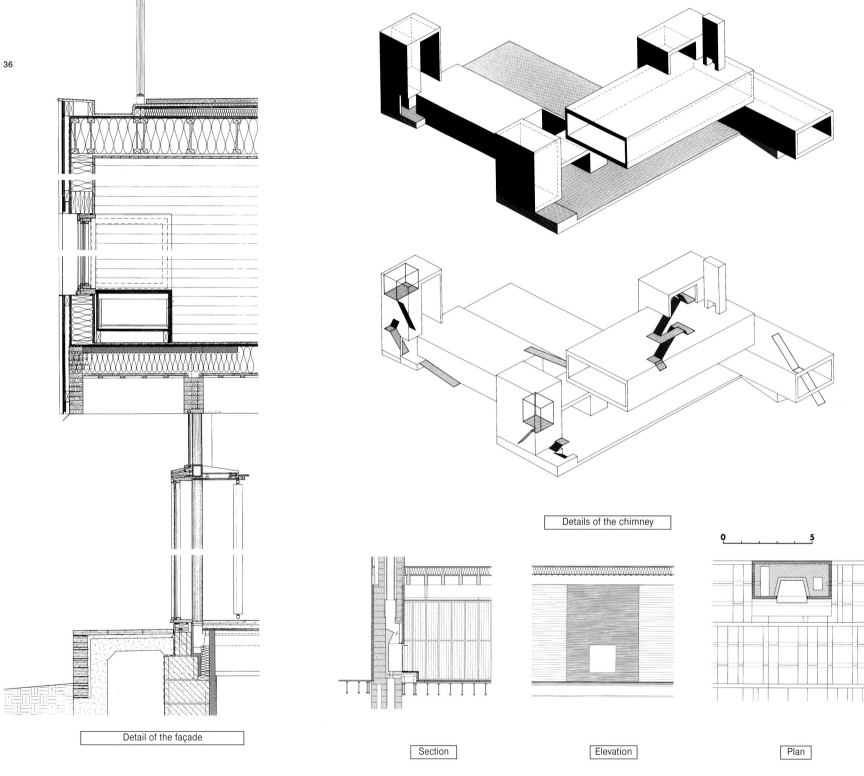

Detail of the façade

Details of the chimney

0   5

Section

Elevation

Plan

38

View of the forest from the corridor.

M House

The M House is a fine example of the flexibility and expertise that characterize projects by this studio, headed by Japanese architect Kazuyo Sejima. Originality and freshness are two outstanding qualities of this dwelling.

The house is located in a fashionable residential neighborhood in downtown Tokyo. It faces the street to the south and has adjacent buildings on three sides. The owners of many of the houses overlooking the street have built walls and drawn curtains for privacy. Given this paradox —having to close what was originally intended to be open— the designers of the M House decided that two fundamental aspects of the project would be harmony with the surroundings and the guarantee of privacy.

The mechanism used to meet these criteria is a sunken patio that provides light and air for the floor below ground, while connecting it to the higher floor, the street, and the sky. The street-level floor is divided crosswise by corridors, stairs, and the patio. It contains the autonomous areas of the house, such as the garage, the double bedroom, and the guest room. The floor below, with a more unified layout arranged around the patio, is characterized by ease of movement from one part to another. The kitchen, dining room, and studio are located on this floor.

The M House was designed with an admirable combination of sensitivity and intelligence. A home of truly impressive beauty, it confirms the status of Kazuyo Sejima and Ryue Nishizawa as Japanese architects who are striving to find solutions to the conflicts of contemporary society by shaking off the preconceptions passed along from generation to generation.

Architects:
    Kazuyo Sejima and Ryue Nishizawa
Photographer:
    Shinkenchiku-Sha
Location:
    Tokyo, Japan
Completion date:
    1997
Floor space:
    2,150 square feet

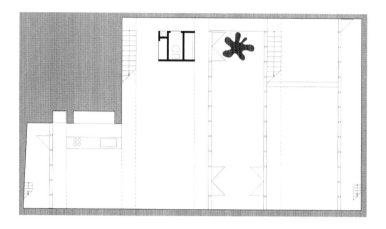

Ground floor

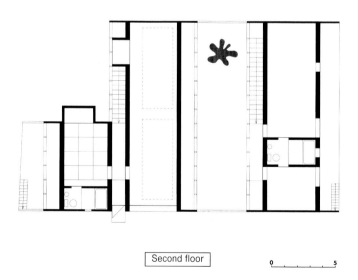

Second floor

0   5

Next page. Two views of the open patio.

View of the library, which is adjacent to the courtyard.

Left. The stair connecting to the upper floor.

B House

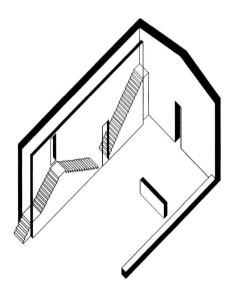

This project involved remodeling an 8,600-square-ft farm building on the edge of a small village halfway between Nice and Aix-en-Provence. In the 18th Century, the building was a resting place for monks and pilgrims headed towards Avignon along an ancient Roman road.

The two-story building was divided lengthwise by a load bearing wall. These original elements were incorporated into the new dwelling which, although quiet and austere without decoration or superficial ornamentation, is nonetheless full of spiritual vitality.

The principal material is stone, used for most of the furniture and the flooring of the entire house. The walls are plaster, painted white. The stone exterior has two entrances which lead to separate rooms.

Solid granary doors open inward to reveal an enormous space containing the living room and a reception area. A 39-ft bench along one wall accentuates the room's length. Above the bench, large curved windows pierce the wall at eye level.

The staircase was envisioned as another wide partition. It goes up and down along the entire length of the house like a corridor, leading to every area. First, it takes you to the guest area, then to the living room, and finally the main bedroom. Placing the staircase between the two compact walls successfully endowed a simple space with cathedral-like magnificence.

In the master bathroom, everything is sculpted in stone: the two sinks are carved in the wall, the shower seems monolithic, and the oval bathtub brings out the stone's sensual charm.

Architects:
    Claudio Silvestrin Architects
Collaborators:
    B. Legal, J.P. Berezinski
Photographer:
    Claudio Silvestrin Architects
Location:
    Provence, France
Completion date:
    1992
Floor space:
    8,600 square feet

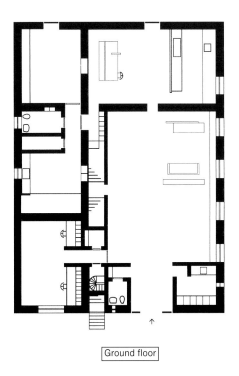

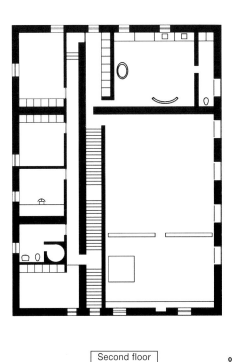

Ground floor

Second floor

0   5

Remodeled stone facades of the old farm in its beautiful surroundings.

The whole bathroom was built in stone.

The furniture was reduced to the minimum.

Y House

This project is located in the residential suburb of the city of Iwakuni, Japan. The architect, Katsufumi Kubota, wanted to clearly differentiate his work from baroque and postmodernist architecture. Here, he has created a truly abstract space where elements without significance disappear.

The objective was to compose pure, transparent environments that establish a connection between people and their surroundings, and that allow them to experience these spaces, reexamining, rediscovering and liberating themselves from the prejudices and tensions inherent in contemporary society. These aims were to be simply and directly achieved using the minium elements possible according to the characteristics of the site and other external considerations like breeze and the movement of the light.

The white box is exposed, perched on top of a mound, allowing the soft breeze in, as well as the brilliant reflected light which contrast with the intense, direct sun beams. The U-shaped concrete volume is made up of one story, a ceiling protecting it and a wall enclosing it. Such simple elements, clearly in response to the characteristics of the land, combine to create and abstract space in which nothing is predetermined.

Architect:
Katsufumi Kubota
Photographer:
N. Nakagawa
Location:
Iwakuni, Yamaguchi, Japan
Completion date:
1997
Floor Space:
4,300 square feet

View of the west façade.

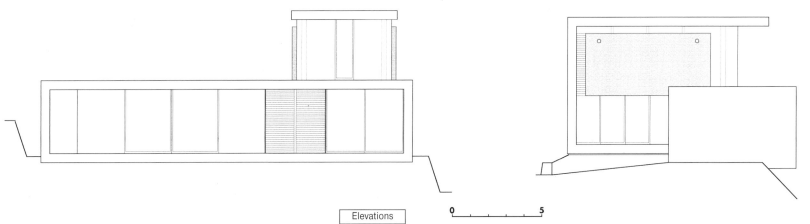

Elevations

0   5

This volume is composed of two U-shaped frames
made of concrete with joints that enhance
transparency. The space is flexible and diaphanous.

The kitchen has nice views to the exterior.

Minimalist Apartment

"Minimalism" is a very broad term which, over the past ten years, has been abused and applied to empty, unfinished, or weak architecture. While its meaning may allow for variations, it is defined by a series of prerequisites that distinguish it from other trends: minimization of formal resources, use of mathematical composition methods – such as serialization or repetition – and, above all, the will to create a particular work whose meaning is not bound to an associated treatise.

Of course, there are different types of Minimalism. On the one hand, some Mediterranean architects have been refining the legacy of the Modern Movement and the vernacular tradition. On the other hand, the austerity of Central European architecture stems from Calvinism, while contemporary Japanese architecture attempts to reinterpret spiritualism. The latter influenced John Pawson during his travels in the East.

The British architect shows that only a few gestures can produce powerful, high-quality designs that need no ornamentation to acquire significance. Although this is a simply described strategy, it requires substantial reductionist efforts.

This project consists of a succession of monumental walls that provide a layout for the apartment which demarcates the smaller, private rooms. The sober texture of the walls and the bone-colored hues provide a solemn, though warm, finish. Horizontal light bathes the vertical partitions, and the light fixtures are disguised to prevent direct visual contact.

The functional plan includes a large, open space for exhibiting works of art and a more private living area. The gallery, library, and living spaces are located in the front of the apartment.

Architect:
John Pawson
Photographer:
Richard Glover
Location:
London, UK
Completion date:
1992
Floor space:
1,600 square feet

These images show the different pieces of furniture made in wood and stone. All of them were designed by the architect's team.

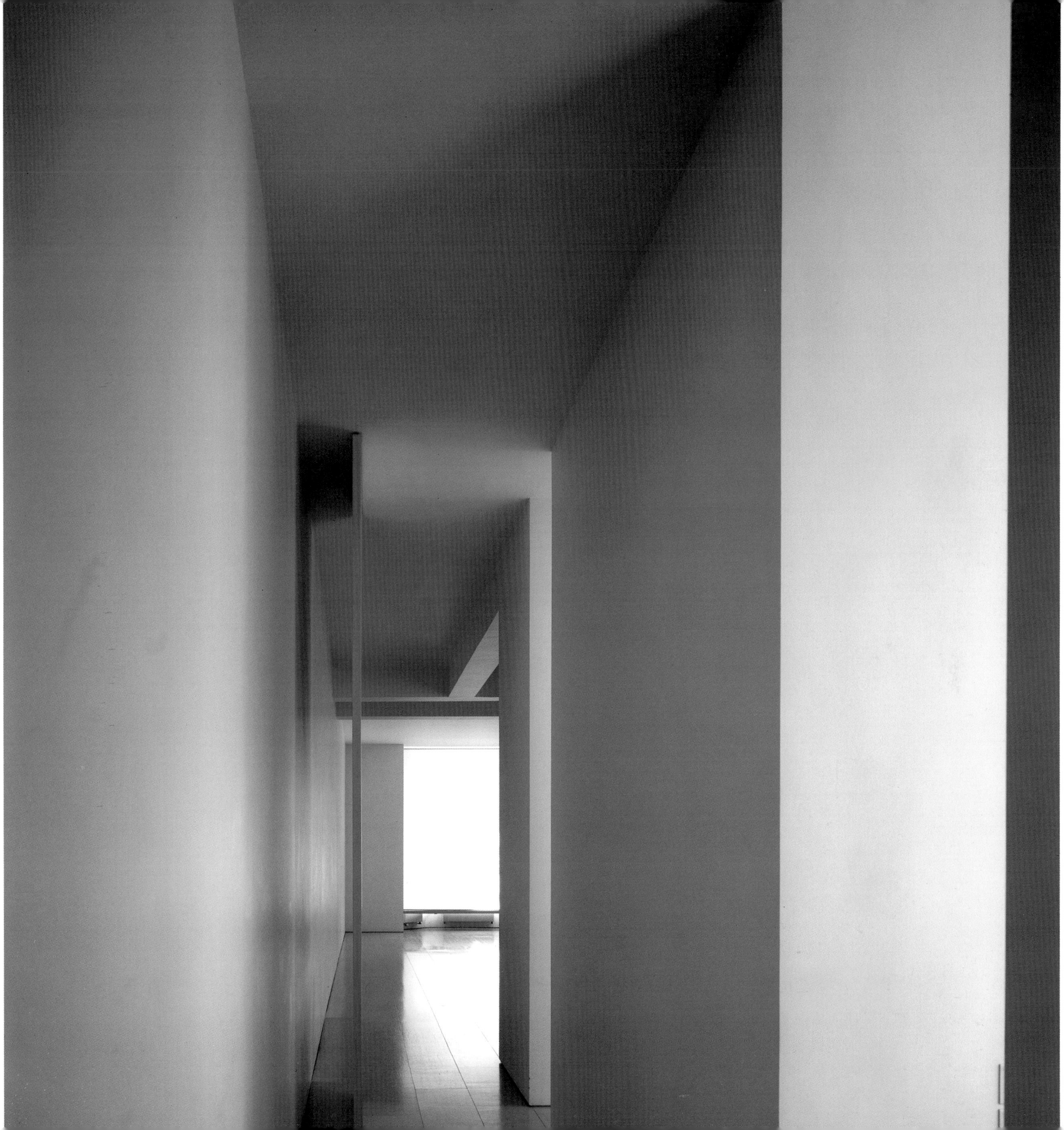

Small, colorful pices of art decorate some of the walls in the interior.

House in Staufen

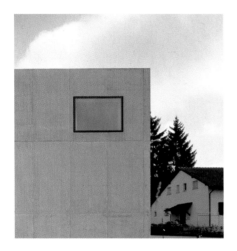

This house is part of an urbanization designed to meet the demand for residences in the area between Geneva and Saint Gallen, in Switzerland. Despite the ecological, landscape an sentimental reservations, the crops which before covered the zone were replaced by homes located near the country's main road and rail networks.

The garden, the only reminder of the past, has key role in this project conditioned by the limited space. At first glance the living areas seem to be one great single room, visible from all the different parts of the house. This area, surrounded by the patio, the porch and the service rooms, opens up to the exterior, the sense of continuity being intensified by the flowing nature of the wood floor and the white walls.

In contrast, the service areas are arranged in compact rooms differentiated by the covering materials, in turn determined by their particular functions. The outside of the building is concrete, clearly distinct from the interior finishes: wood in the entrance, glass mosaic in the bathroom, fabrics around the dressing room and the black paint in the kitchen which evokes the soot of the old chimneys.

Architect:
Morger & De
Photographer:
Ruedi Walti
Location:
Staufen, S
Completion date
1999
Floor space:
1,000 squa

Above. View of the entrance façade with no
windows but one that lights the bedroom.
Right. Detail of the glass windows of the courtyard.

The main bathroom.

Right. A glass porch
gives access to the small pool.

Panoramic House

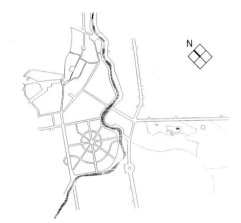

In the various minimalist disciplines -painting, sculpture, architecture, and literature- the aim is to be highly expressive with as few gestures as possible. Consequently, there are always few lines, but these few are forceful, giving the work its character. In some cases the minimization of ideas is taken to the limit and a fundamental aspect is omitted to highlight other issues and bring the absent element into focus. This house, designed by Aranda, Pigem and Vilalta, is a fine example. The architects rejected all superficial elements that would cloud perception of the space without adding quality and specificity.

The stunning beauty of the landscape called for a project that would focus attention on the magnificent countryside. The house sits atop a gentle slope and looks like a floating observation post. With the lines of a pavilion, the steelwork and roof set off the building's large glass panels. A glass base connects the house with the ground, reinforcing the floating sensation and allowing light to pass into the semi-basement.

The house's entrance is in the open area between the two volumes which comprise the residence. One section contains the service area, and the other, the bedrooms and living areas. High ceilings and other open spaces connect the project's different environments and permit the rooms to flow together.

In minimalist architecture, building details play a very low-key role. They are merely tools to give expression to the materials and textures. This project, which blends impeccable stone surfaces and glass façades, is in a class by itself in terms of the play of light and the views inside. However, what makes these subtle perceptions possible is the perfect construction that focuses complete attention on the house's abstract, immaterial elements.

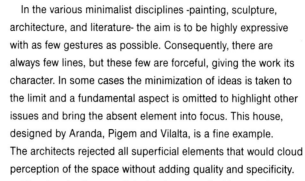

Architects:
    Aranda, Pigem
Collaborators:
    A. Saez, M. T
    Margui
Photographer:
    Eugeni Pons
Location:
    Olot, Spain
Completion date:
    1999
Floor space:
    square

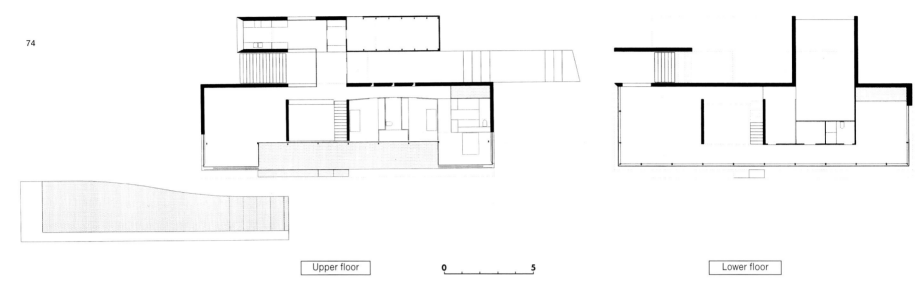

Upper floor

0   5

Lower floor

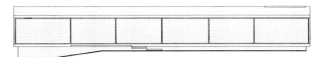

Elevations

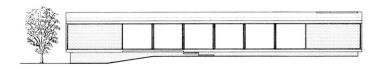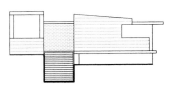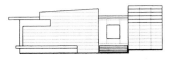

Elevations

0 ___ 5

The impressive main façade.

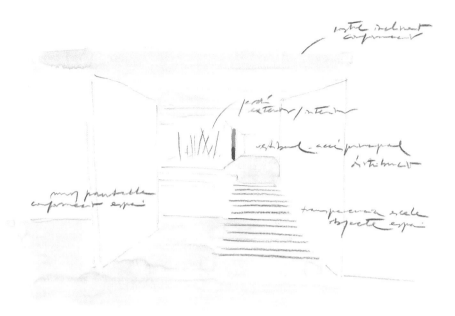

Original sketches by the architects

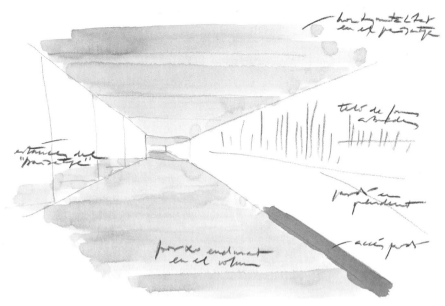

Two views of the lower floor.

Graf Offices

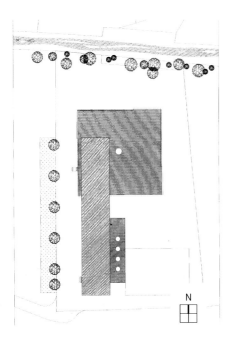

When the original Graf electric company building had to be expanded, the decision was made to attach two independent modules that would form a compact corporate complex. The clients wanted it to have a strong visual impact on its setting, with the new structures being clearly recognizable within a perfectly unified whole.

The conditions were difficult and delicate. The existing office building was not particularly attractive and the soil conditions imposed limitations. The phreatic water level was very high and there were gravel layers down to 1,000 feet. Both factors complicated the design of the concrete structures and foundations.

Transportation and communication considerations dictated that production and warehouse facilities be placed in a square at ground level. To unite the complex, this was connected to the original building by a bridge, a representational structure housing the firm's administrative offices.

Wooden slats were affixed to the exterior of the original building to achieve an aesthetic compositional balance. The new bridge construction, in glass and colored concrete, looks like a beam running across the light-filled windows below it. Geological constraints meant that heavy loads could not be placed on top of the original building. This problem was solved by constructing adjacent foundations.

The concrete's bold orange color makes the offices visible from far away, almost as an advertisement for the electric company. The bridge-beam design permits plenty of windows with maximum height and width. Inside, the reinforced concrete was painted white and left exposed to emphasize the beam's function.

Architects:
Baumschlager & Eberle
Collaborators:
Reinhard Drexel, Ernst Mader
Photographer:
Eduard Hueber
Location:
Dornbirn, Austria
Completion date:
1995
Floor space:
14,000 square feet

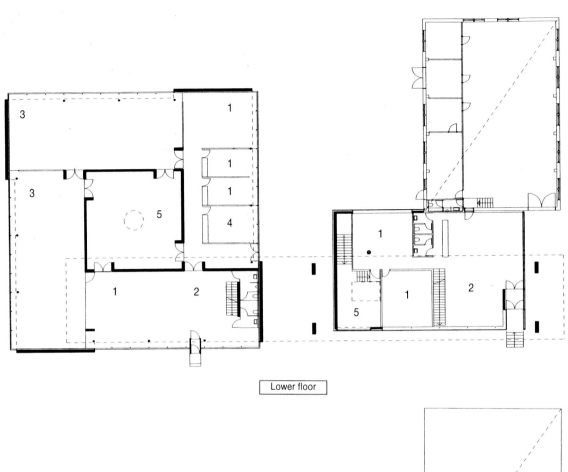

1. Office
2. Reception
3. Workshop
4. Boardroom
5. Storage

Lower floor

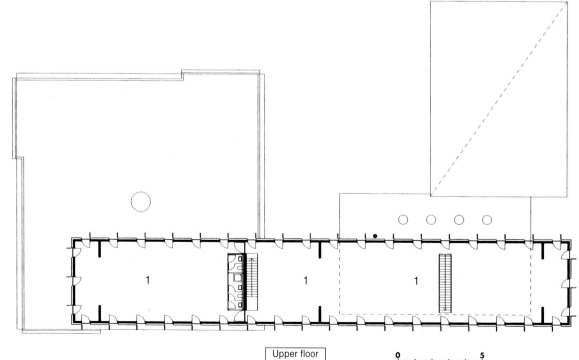

Upper floor

0   5

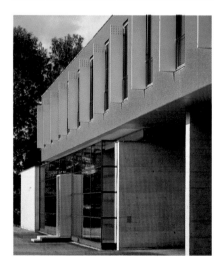

Bathing Pavilion

Though the pavilion frequently appears in architectural terminology, architects rarely build them. Pavilions are among the most complicated building types because their success depends on their transparency. Designers often succumb to the sentimental idea of a pavilion and apply their precepts to other works. They are isolated, impermanent, and permeable. They should not obstruct the view and should encourage people to wander through them. Mies Van der Rohe and Phillip Johnson have created magnificent examples.

The functional requirements of this project gave Aranda, Pigem, and Vilalta certain latitude in designing this landmark in the middle of a park in the province of Girona, Spain. Their goal was to show nature as a combination of the landscape and the man-made environment. The result is a small building conceived as a sculpture, a work of "Land Art" in an exceptional setting.

The pavilion is located at the top of a gentle slope, lightly poised on the land as if it were floating. The slight difference in height between the pavilion's platform and the hillside provides drainage and makes it possible to sit on the edge and enjoy fine views of the nearby river.

The subtle curvature of the pavilion assimilates the natural setting into the project and varies the perspectives of the landscape framed by the building's components. These spaces offer splendid views enhanced by the reflections and luminosity of the smooth, shiny pavement.

With the Bathing Pavilion, the architects were able to experiment with construction on a small, human scale. In doing so, they made the structural elements as unobtrusive as possible. The thinness of the roof, especially the eaves, is a clear example of this technique.

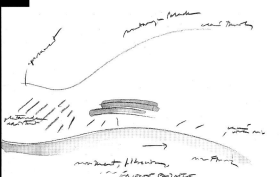

Architects:
    Aranda, Pigem & V

Collaborators:
    A. Saez, A. Blazq
    M. Subiras

Photographer:
    Eugeni Pons

Location:
    Olot, Spain

Completion date:
    1998

Floor space:
    1,300 square feet

View of the pavilion in its magnificent setting.

92

Detail of the pavilion's bathrooms.

Ridaura's Civic Center

N

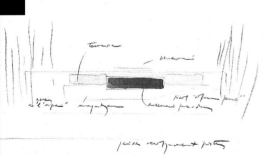

The small village of Ridaura, located in a valley in the province of Girona, Spain, has 800 inhabitants. Formerly, the school occupied the first floor of a house, and the only public buildings were the church and the village hall. Due to the lack of space for community activities, the decision was made to build a center in which different cultural, leisure, and sports events could be held. A plot of land near the entrance to the village and the church was chosen as the site.

One of the project's principal objectives, and an obsession of the young architects involved, was respect for the environment, modifying the site without harming it. The challenge was to design a flexible civic center that could be used for various social activities while blending in with the ambience of the old village and the countryside.

The architects designed a horizontal parallelepiped which would reinforce the vertical axis of the church. The building, modest in size, lies across the plot in order to accommodate a plaza in front of it. Behind the building, a larger area is used as a playground and for dances and sports. The two open-air spaces are connected by a series of deep, shady porches that form part of the building.

What makes Ridaura's Civic Center unique is the contrast between the modern lines of the building and its agrarian, traditional surroundings. Aranda, Pigem, and Vilalta did not want to renounce contemporary architecture by yielding to the village's more rustic look. The skylights, stages, arcades, and viewpoints give the building its personality and make it suitable for varied activities. The interior is filled with natural light, which flows through the large glass windows and skylights.

Architects:
Aranda, Pigem & Vilalta
Collaborators:
A. Saez, A. Blazquez, I
Subiras
Photographer:
Eugeni Pons
Location:
Ridaura, Girona, Spain
Completion date:
1999
Floor space:
5,400 square feet

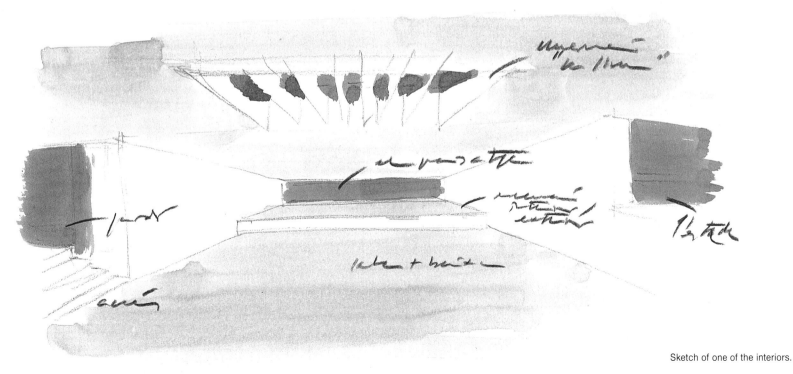

Sketch of one of the interiors.

View of the building and the open space used for activities.

The benches in the entrance hall were also designed by the architects.

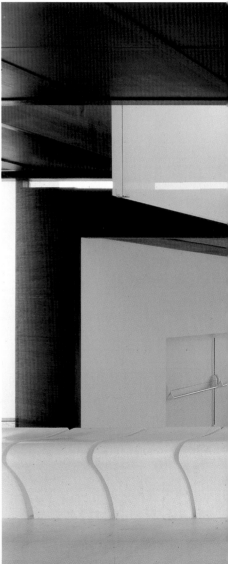

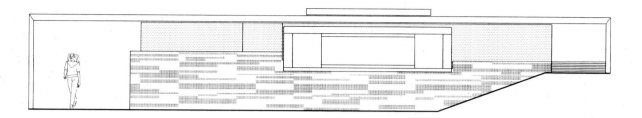

Section

0 — — — 5

Law School

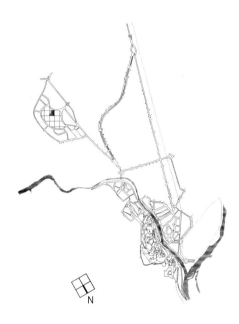

The most distinctive characteristics of these architects based in the small town of Olot, in Spain, are emphatic components, an abundant variety of open space, impeccable control of natural light, the ability to emphasize or conceal certain aspects of a building, and precision in structural detail. This Law School, on the Montilivi Campus on the outskirts of Girona, Spain, manifests each of these qualities.

The plot's steep slope was a challenge that the architects had to overcome. A hard, blunt base separates the building from the land, preserving its autonomy.

The project cleverly combines occupied and unoccupied spaces, the latter being comprised of open-air patios and terraces, and two-story interior passages and walkways. The richness of these areas stems from the materials: nearly sensual finishes and a multiplicity of textures that reflect light in a variety of ways. The overall effect almost makes you forget you are in a man-made structure.

The functional interior layout does not emerge on the exterior. Each face employs the same material, which lets natural light enter uniformly, giving the building an integrated appearance. In fact, only the vertical slits that provide light for the interior patios interrupt the constancy of the building's faces.

The Law School is the result of an intricate creative process engendered by the site, its setting, and the very specific functional requirements. The architects' genius lies in the creation of a building that is conducive to campus life while pleasing the senses.

Architects:
Aranda, Pigem & Vilalta
Collaborators:
A. Saez, M. Tàpies, W. Wein
Photographer:
Eugeni Pons
Location:
Girona, Spain
Completion date:
1999
Floor space:
13,000 square feet

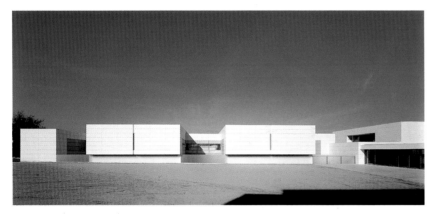

Typical floor

0   5

Next page. Two-story interior passages and walkways.

No Picnic Offices

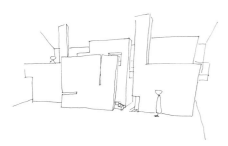

No Picnic, a Swedish industrial design firm, hired Claesson, Koivisto, and Rune to completely renovate the firm's headquarters in a 1930's industrial building. The architects considered it fundamental to design a dynamic, open plan in line with the company's creative nature.

However, the firm also required more intimate spaces where confidentiality could be maintained. Accordingly, the architects created three different levels: the basement for the technical section, the ground floor for rooms used by the various staff members – reception area, kitchen, meeting rooms, and workshop – and finally, the second floor, where privacy for projects could be ensured.

Despite the clearly defined layout, the architects regarded the project as a labyrinth because of the way the staircase divided the space. The staircase, in the center of the building and parallel to the façade, narrows as it stretches upwards, combining strong visual impact with a design rooted in Dutch Neoplasticism.

The partitions demarcating the staircase vary in height according to the needs of the offices alongside. Various horizontal and vertical openings were cut into the partitions and covered with glass. The staircase's importance lies in the fact that it articulates the spaces, defines the levels, and, at the ground floor entry, separates the working area from the other rooms.

The workshop, in which models are constructed, has a two-story ceiling. This brightens the room and recalls the building's industrial past.

Architects:
Claesson Koivisto
Rune Arkitektkontor

Collaborator:
Christiane Bosse

Photographer:
Patrik Engquist

Location:
Stockholm, Sweden

Completion date:
1997

Floor space:
4,850 square feet

108

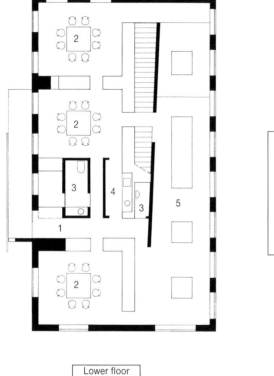

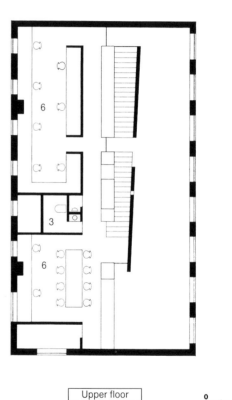

1. Entrance

2. Boardroom

3. Bathroom

4. Kitchen

5. Workshop

6. Project room

Lower floor

Upper floor

0   5

Previous page. The staircase was designed following the trends of Dutch Neoplasticism.

Right. Partial views of one of the boardrooms.

110

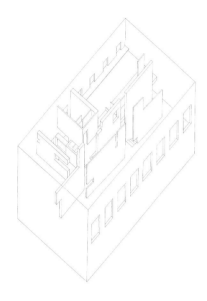

Main entrance.

Above. View of the kitchen and the open walls at the back.

Osho International Offices

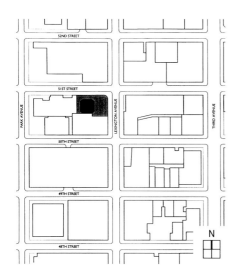

This project involved the New York headquarters of an international publishing company specializing in subjects related to Zen and meditation. The goal was to create an office environment that would reflect the spirit of the individuals who work there and the particular ideas the company embraces.

The offices occupy the 46th floor of the former GE tower on New York's Lexington Avenue. This tall, slender building has an unusually small floor plan of just 3,000 square feet, with the building systems and elevator core located on the skyscraper's south side.

The office design is anchored by the consolidation of the elevator lobby, reception desk, and conference area into one large space. This central, communal room is defined by floor-to-ceiling storage and media cabinets on two sides, 55-foot translucent glass wall on the side facing the elevators. This laminated wall is acid-etched on one side and polished on the other. From the entrance, one can make out the movements and shadows of the individuals inside the office. On the hallway side, the glass reflects the activity in the inner offices, emphasizing their private nature.

The underlying agenda in all project-related decisions (planning, materials, details, and composition) was to be reductive in nature, quiet in spirit, and consistent in execution. The intention was to create a meditative landscape that would stimulate creativity yet offer a reprieve from the energy and influence of midtown Manhattan.

Architect:
    Daniel Rowen
Photographer:
    Michael Mora
Location:
    New York City
Completion date:
    1998
Floor space:
    3,000 square

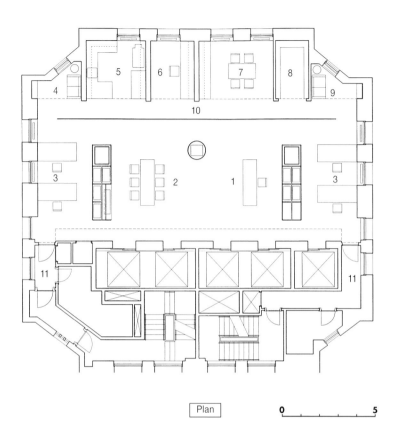

Plan

0   5

1. Reception
2. Conference
3. Workstations
4. West lounge
5. Work room
6. Audio room
7. Video room
8. Archive room
9. East lounge
10. Hall of reflection
11. Service corridor

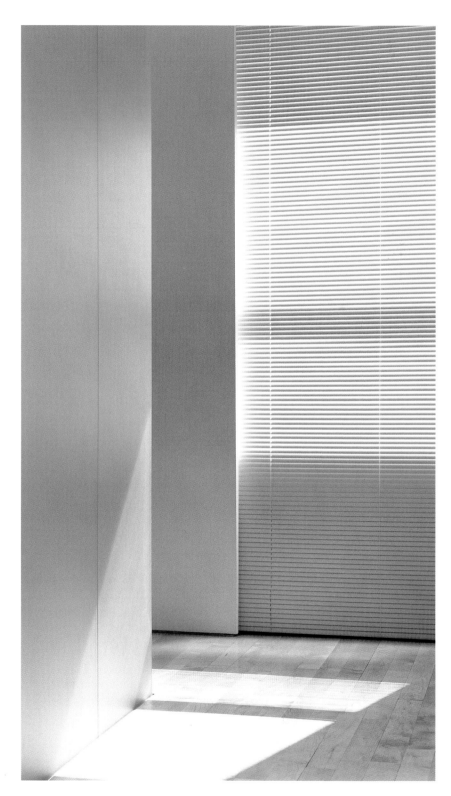

116

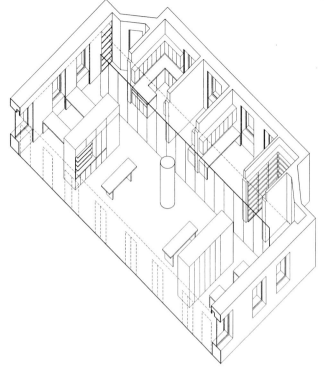

Axonometric view of half of the project.

Views of the entrance hall and the meeting room.

Architecture Studio

The offices of GCA Architects is woven into Barcelona's smooth urban fabric, occupying former textile warehouses on the ground floor of a building constructed in 1946.

In the textile tradition, it was common to place the offices at the front, beneath the rest of the building, with the warehouses at the back, occupying the remainder of the space. Typically, there were classically inspired, compartmentalized offices located beside the entry, with cornices and moldings. The interior consisted of an open space supported by metal trusses and columns.

Faced with this traditional arrangement, the architects adopted a dual strategy. First, they preserved the appearance of the existing offices by restoring the woodwork, and they designed reception, administration, and management areas. Then, in the former warehouse area, they created a clearly modern space devoted to design. The project was based on a dialogue between opposites, but the working area plays by far the leading role. Conceived as a large white box lit from above by two huge skylights, the plan reflects the gestation process of architectural work (projects and drafting room, project management office,...). This sequence ends at a large exterior patio.

Light is the fundamental element. White walls, maple floors, and glass partitions form a homogeneous, minimalist expanse in which spatial limits disappear while a multiplicity of views and perspectives are introduced.

Architects:
   GCA Arquitectes Associats
Collaborators:
   CODECSA (builder), Gerelec (electri
   and lighting), Ebanistería Pomar (w
   work), CLIMATERM (air conditioning)
Photographer:
   Jordi Miralles
Location:
   Barcelona, Spain
Completion date:
   1996
Floor space:
   10,750 square feet

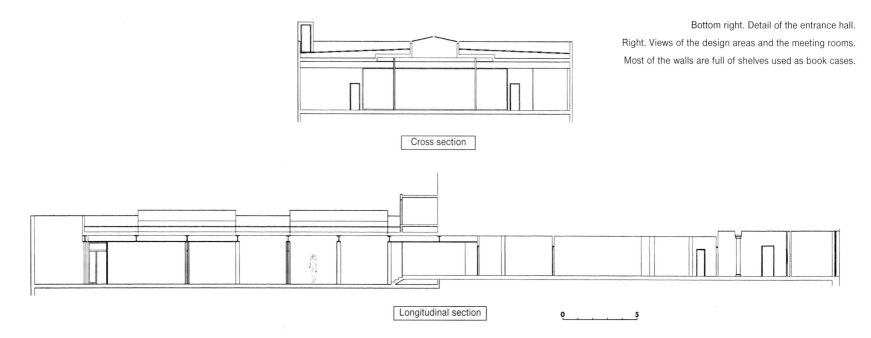

Cross section

Longitudinal section

0 _____ 5

Bottom right. Detail of the entrance hall.

Right. Views of the design areas and the meeting rooms.

Most of the walls are full of shelves used as book cases.

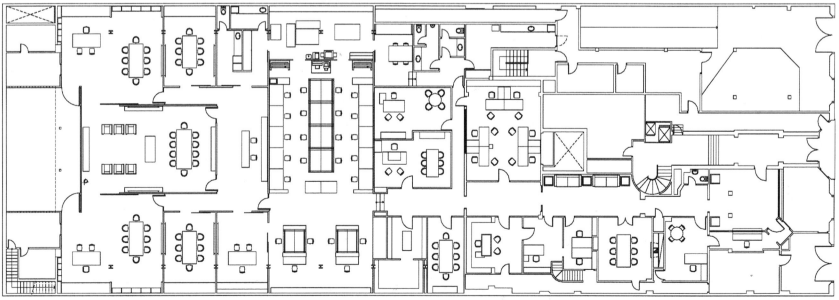

General ground plan

Information Center

The task of this project was to remodel the English Sports Council's reception area, enhancing the professional image of this governmental organization while making the entrance a friendly place welcoming visitors and staff. Since it is a public institution, the contract was awarded after a highly competitive selection process.

Once the architects had been chosen, the team worked on the details in close collaboration with the client to ensure that the entire reception area reflected the building's purpose as a provider of useful information.

The area has two parts, one semi-private and the other public, separated by a wall that encloses the facilities and services. The façade is made of glass because the designers wanted nothing, not even a frame, to restrict the view of what was going on inside the building. The new exhibition gallery, with a stainless steel framework for displays of photography, art, and architecture, with a large video screen on one partition, is clearly visible from the street. Therefore, one encounters the informational role of the reception area even before entering the building.

There are more views: the walls of the facility has openings so employees can see the street and visitors can observe the office layout.

Simon Conder Associates, took charge of the entire construction process, right down to the design of the furniture and the method for mounting exhibits. With the limited project size, this approach allowed the architects to effectively accomplish the assigned task.

Architects:
    Simon Conder Associates
Photographers:
    Chris Gascoigne and Nathan Willoc
Location:
    London, England
Completion date:
    1998
Floor space:
    2,500 square feet

Axonometric view of the project.

Top. View of the reception hall.

Bottom. Detail of the exhibition panels on the entrance wall.

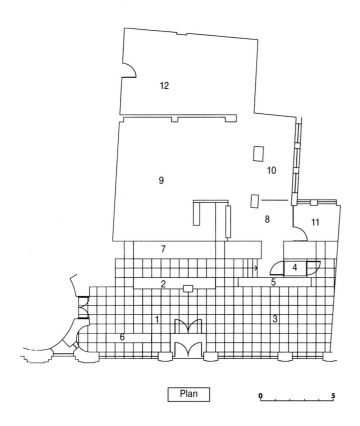

12

9

10

8

11

7

4

2

5

1

3

6

Plan

0   5

1. Reception

2. Reception desk

3. Gallery

4. Handicapped elevator

5. Video wall

6. Bench

7. Storage Wall

8. Information

9. Library

10. Reading area

11. Office

12. Open plan offices

Crematorium in Berlin

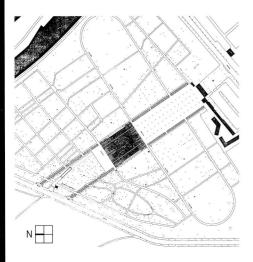

This building's specialized function as the city's crematorium played the key role in the design process. The architects understood that the building's objective was not to change the visitor's mood but to provide a suitable environment for gatherings, reflection, and meditation, a place of rest where silence would predominate. Religious architecture and mysticism provided inspiration for the project and helped define the abstract requirements of a space designed for saying one's final good-byes.

The building contains references to ancient structures. For example, a *piazza coperta* (covered square) forms the central meeting point, leading off to several large rooms. Lighting, an important element in creating the ambience, is carefully focused in the hall. Stone columns reach up to the ceiling, forming hollow spaces through which the sun shines. More light enters through gaps between the walls and ceiling. Artificial spotlights intensify both effects.

Three principal materials were used: concrete, glass, and metal slats, which cover most of the windows. A powerful statement is made by the large concrete surfaces and the dialogue between the massiveness of the façade and its openings, especially on the south face. The metal blinds filter and soften the light, bringing warmth to the rooms.

Axel Shultes' and Charlotte Frank's crematorium is a monumental, solemn building that nonetheless manages to provide a welcoming ambience. The building is effective: workers and visitors alike benefit from the tranquil atmosphere made possible by the various structural elements.

Architects:
Axel Shultes + Charlotte Frank
Collaborators:
Margret Kister, Christoph Witt
Photographer:
Reinhard Görner/Artur
Location:
Berlin, Germany
Completion date:
1998
Floor space:
100,500 square feet

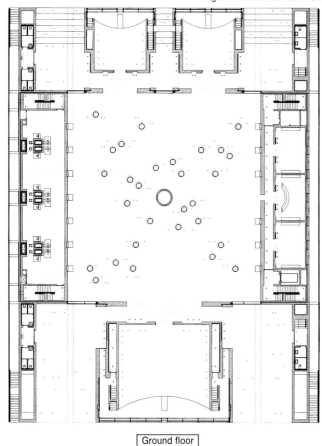

Right. Metal blinds filter the natural light.

Ground floor

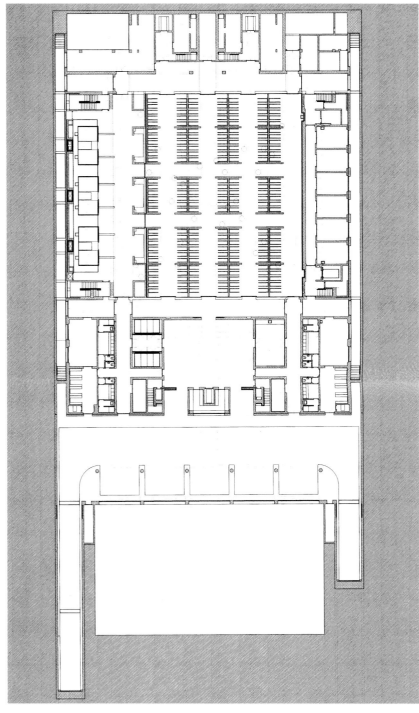

Basement

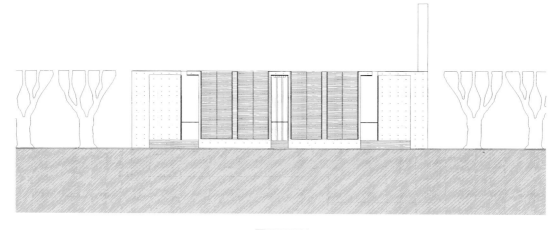

Elevation

Stone columns reach up to the ceiling in the covered square.

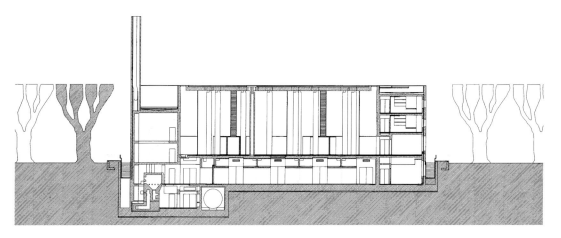

Section

View of the central meeting point.

Bang and Olufsen Offices

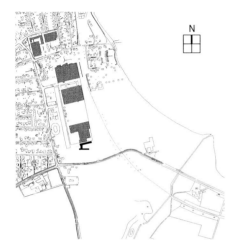

N

An intense dialogue between Bang and Olufsen and the architects gave the client such confidence that the architects were granted total freedom to choose the project's guiding principles and design details.

The only requirement was that it be a flagship building that would perfectly express the company's identity. Opulence and ostentation were to be avoided, and the project had to stay within a modest budget.

The remote, isolated farms that dot the Danish countryside inspired the building design. These farmhouses have a courtyard, or patio, which allows visual contact among the different parts of the building. Bang and Olufsen wanted their headquarters, like these traditional structures, to engender harmony among their enterprise, the structural technology, and the countryside's poetic dimension. To avoid spoiling the vulnerable beauty of the surrounding landscape and the old rural houses, the new building was designed to be light, transparent, and unobtrusive.

In contrast to the placid setting, the building's interior is complex, since it must integrate all the different activities that take place in the various areas. Upon entering the building, one sees a multiplicity of different environments. Placing the corridors and stairs along the façade facilitates communication and visibility among the workers.

Although the components of the headquarters are geometrically simple, their union and juxtaposition create rich spatial variations intricately related to the landscape. The combination of different materials highlights this effect. Basalt, glass, concrete, and wood flooring define the various spaces, making other dividing lines, such as walls and doors, unnecessary.

Architects:
    KHR AS
Collaborators:
    Birch & Krog
Photographers:
    Ib Sørensen
Location:
    Struer, Denma
Completion date:
    1998
Floor space:
    55,400 squar

134

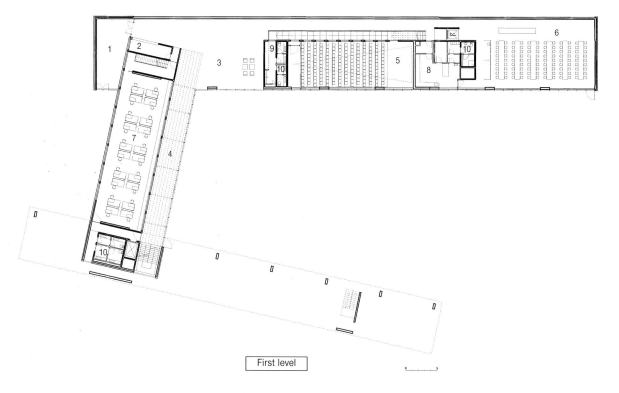

First level

1. Entrance
2. Reception
3. Hall
4. Corridor
5. Auditorium
6. Dining room
7. Offices
8. Kitchen
9. Wardrobe
10. Restrooms

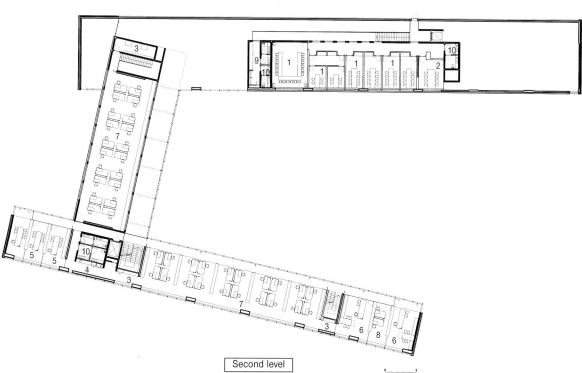

Second level

1. Conference room
2. Dining room
3. Copy room
4. Kitchen
5. Main office
6. Director's office
7. Offices
8. Secretary's office
9. Wardrobe
10. Restrooms

Exterior views in which the beautiful surrounding countryside can be seen.

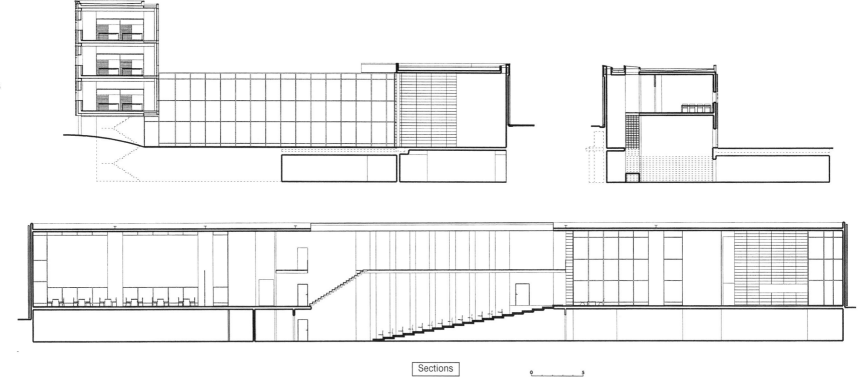

Sections

0   5

View of the dining room.

Corridors and stairs run along the main façade.

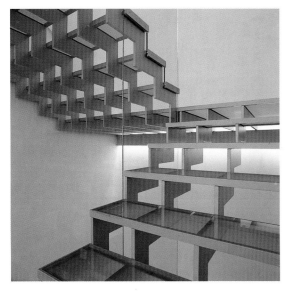

Antonio Pernas Boutique

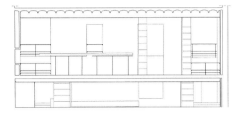

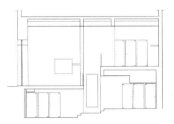

These refurbished premises designed by Iago Seara house the sales outlet for a specific product: women's clothing by the designer Antonio Pernas. The architect wanted not only to create a functional space, but also to establish a connection between the style of clothing on display and the type of woman for whom it is intended.

A boutique has to be a "spatial logo" of the firm it represents and the merchandise being sold. The setting must encapsulate the company's philosophy and reinforce the product's image, targeted to a very specific market.

To achieve this, the renovated boutique, like the clothing on sale, uses the textures and finishes of natural materials, such as wood and stone. Given the kinds of products on sale and the women who will wear them, the project had to respond to the success of the "Modern Movement" and the demands of contemporary architecture.

The two stories (basement and ground floor) are divided into four levels, with a space spanning both stories which, along with the open-sided staircase, visually links the entire store.

The façade was preserved in its original state, although there was some additional woodwork. Inside, the floors are made of stone from Alicante, Spain, and the prefabricated vertical partitions are plasterboard.

Lighting was one of the trickiest aspects since, as in other Antonio Pernas boutiques, it plays a key role in defining the spaces. Light can point out, enhance, or highlight a product on sale, while creating a pleasant ambience that encourages shopping.

Architect:
Iago Seara
Photographer:
Eugeni Pons
Location:
Barcelona, Spain
Completion date:
1998
Floor space:
4,600 square feet

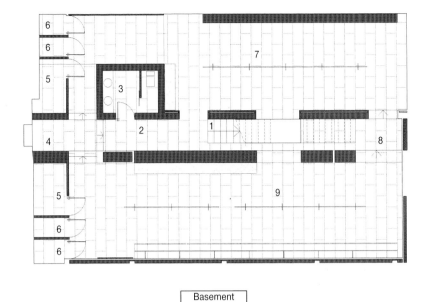

Basement

1. Staircase
2. Corridor
3. Restroom
4. Broom closet
5. Storage rooms
6. Basement fitting rooms
7. Sales floor
8. Passageway
9. Sales floor

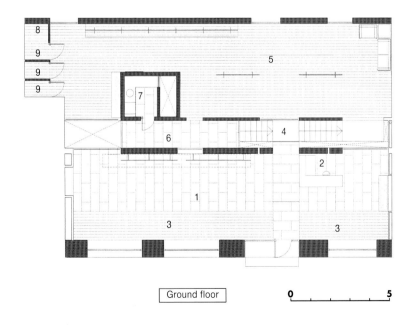

Ground floor

0   5

1. Entrance and
   display area
2. Cashier area
3. Shop window
4. Staircase
5. Sales floor
6. Corridor
7. Office
8. Storage room
9. First floor fitting rooms

Basement sales floor where the original vaulted ceiling can be seen.

Right. The basement locates the sales floors,
fitting rooms, storage and some display areas.

Wagamama Restaurant

Wagamama, a Japanese restaurant, occupies the ground floor and basement of a wide but shallow building in the heart of London's Soho district.

Surprisingly, the dining room is in the basement, with the kitchen on the ground floor. The design by David Chipperfield Architects pays special attention to the customer's progression from street to table. Seven of the eight existing recesses in the façade were filled with fixed glass panels. This provides a view of the dining room from the street through a basement-to-ground floor space running the length of the building. The eighth recess is the entrance.

Three stairways lead to the ground floor, which is slightly above street level. Once inside, customers wait in a long corridor where they can watch food being prepared in the kitchen. At the other end of the corridor, an acid-treated glass screen separates customers waiting to be taken to their tables from the long, two-story space and the street. At night, the patrons' silhouettes are outlined on the screen.

In the dining room, a series of long wooden tables and stools runs perpendicular to the access corridor and the double-story space. Food descends from the kitchen in anodized aluminum dumb waiters and is then carried to the tables. In the rear of the dining room, counters display desserts, juices, and drinks; under the stairs, another counter shows items for sale.

Architects:
    David Chipperfield

Collaborators:
    Overbury Interiors
    Chan Associates (s
    BSC Consulting Eng
    engineering); Tim
    (supervisor).

Photographer:
    Richard Davies

Location:
    London, UK

Completion date:
    1996

Floor space:
    11,000 square feet

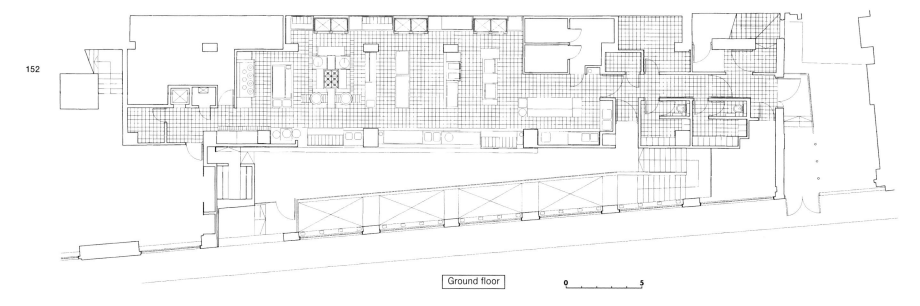

Ground floor

0 _____ 5

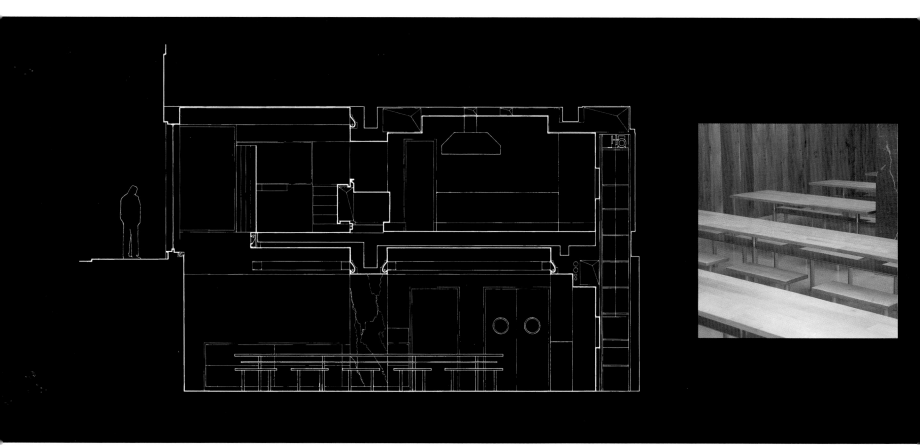

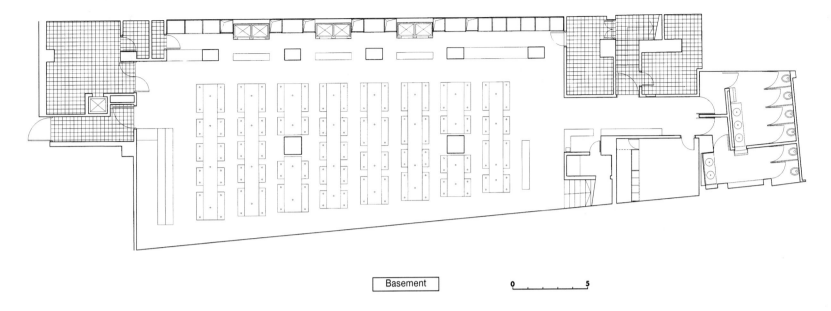

Basement   0 ____ 5

The dining room is full of long wooden tables.

One Happy Cloud Restaurant

Traditional Japanese culture shares two characteristics with Scandinavian architecture: an interest in how light is dealt with and a quest for design simplicity. The developer of One Happy Cloud, a Japanese restaurant in Stockholm, did not want his establishment to be merely a picturesque place for serving sushi. Rather, the idea was to create a place where Japanese and Scandinavian traditions would merge in both gastronomic and aesthetic terms.

The result is a venue of extraordinary simplicity and elegance. There are no direct references to Japanese culture. Instead, there are subtle allusions to the quiet, relaxing atmosphere of the country's typical architecture. The nearly square, approximately 1600-square-foot restaurant has a dining area arranged in two narrow rooms which together form an L shape. The remainder of the space contains the kitchen and restrooms.

The tables line the restaurant's perimeter. Existing walls and large, acid-etched glass partitions divide the rooms into smaller, more private areas. The walls are plastered and painted white, with the exception of the one behind the bar, which features chalk drawings on a black background by graphics designer Nill Svensson. The rooms' considerable height in relation to their width, the plain, white vertical panels, the translucent partitions, the absence of decorative elements, and the simple, solid furniture in matte-varnished beechwood all contribute to the image of restraint, so pleasing yet so evanescent.

Architects:
    Claesson Koivisto Rune Arkitektkontor
Collaborators:
    Christiane Bosse, Mattias Stahlbom
    (assistants), New World Inredning AB
    (contractor), Ralambshovs Snikerier AB
    (woodwork), Nybergs Glas AB (glass)
Photographer:
    Patrik Engquist
Location:
    Stockholm, Sweden
Completion date:
    1997
Floor space:
    1,600 square feet

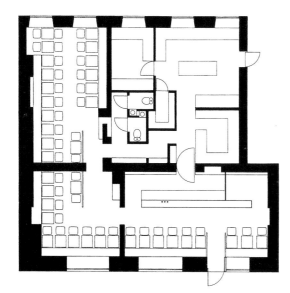

Ground plan

0   5

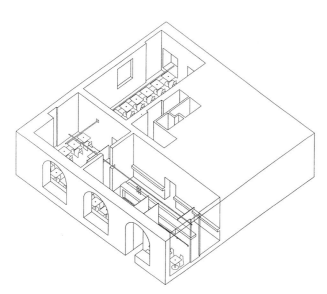

Axonemetric view.

View of restaurant, bar and the chalk drawing on the back wall.

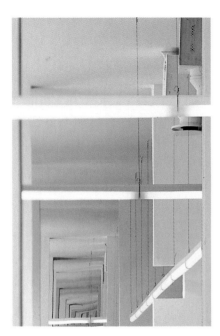

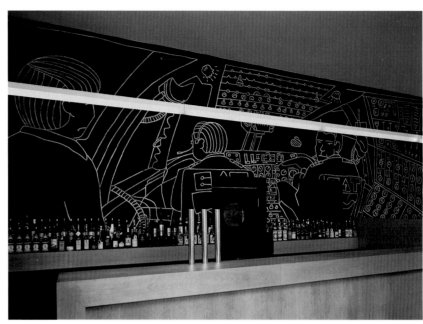

The flooring is polished gray cement.

Julie Sohn Boutique

This project is located on the first floor of a building in Barcelona's Ensanche district, a neighborhood that is turning around as it attracts more and more businesses. The property is a perfect example of the street level commercial premises found in this area: a narrow front in a long, deep building with at least a 13-foot ceiling.

The project's guiding concept was the creation of an open, neutral space where clothes could be displayed like works of art, a concept inspired by nearby art galleries on the same side of the street.

The shop had to be in keeping with the image the owners were trying to create for their line of clothing. One *sine qua non* was concealment of all air-conditioning and lighting units.

The architects were faced with a property resembling a tube which becomes progressively wider towards the interior. The depth of the premises and the high ceilings contrasted with the narrow front. To make the back part as spacious as possible, one of the structural walls was taken down.

The building's façade was left unaltered, although a glass front was installed, set back slightly at an angle to avoid reflections and highlight the entrance.

The interior walls and ceilings were covered with two layers of plasterboard to prevent problems with humidity and structural movement. Matte stainless steel was used for the handles, baseboards, and hangers.

To consolidate the property's strange shape, all interior surfaces, including the unbroken concrete flooring, were painted white. A box-like plaster structure mediates between the ceiling and walls and conceals the lights, speakers, and air vents.

Architects:
    Conrado Carrasco and Carlos Tejada
Photographer:
    Eugeni Pons
Location:
    Barcelona, Spain
Completion date:
    1997
Floor space:
    1,378 square feet

View of the shop from the street.

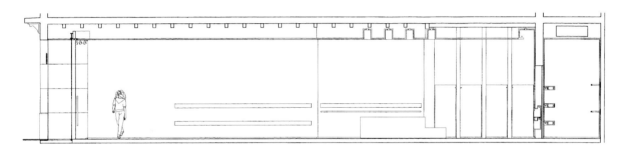

Section

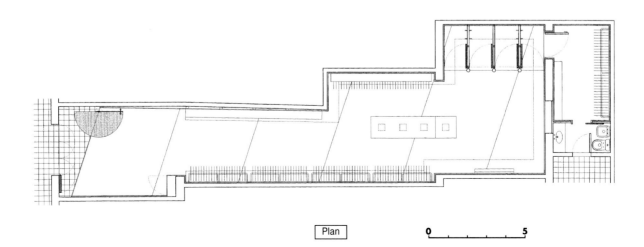

Plan

0 ____ 5

Views of the shop from each end.

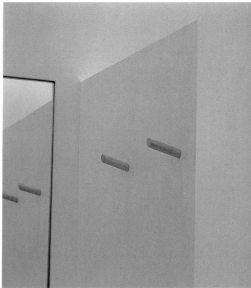

View and detail of the fitting rooms.

A jewelry store in Munich

Minimalism is not simply negation, subtraction, or puritanism. It can be defined as reducing architecture to the basic concepts of space, light, and mass. While minimalism dispenses with decoration, it celebrates form and space. This project by Landau & Kindelbacher is a good example. It demonstrates how apparently simple architecture can mask a project's profound complexity.

The jewelry store, in a post-war building in a Munich commercial district, has a display and sales area, along with a workshop for designing and producing pieces for the various collections. The showroom's high ceiling makes it an ideal place to exhibit jewelry.

The architects decided not to divide the space in a traditional manner. The partition separating the workshop from the store was opened up to allow full visual communication.
The transparency of the exhibition areas and the gray of the walls and flooring emphasize the depth of the premises.

The display cases were specially designed. The largest is a stainless steel case containing a glass-enclosed shelf, on which the items can be viewed. A counter on wheels, with the cash register and several drawers, can be pulled out of it.

Another display cabinet, made of maple, pivots on a fixed steel post. The showcases are made of steel with glass at the front and back, so the jewelry can be seen without blocking the view through the store from outside.

The carefully-planned lighting maintains subtlety while highlighting the pieces. There are small spotlights in the ceiling, although halogen tubes in the cabinets illuminate the jewels.

Architects:
    Landau & Kir

Collaborator:
    Lene Jünger

Photographer:
    Michael Heir

Location:
    Munich, Germ

Completion date:
    1997

Floor space:
    1,775 square

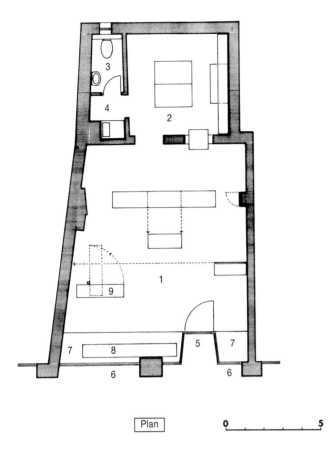

Plan

0 ____ 5

1. Display area
2. Workshop
3. Toilet
4. Washroom
5. Entrance
6. Shop window
7. Display area
8. Display case
9. Pivoting display cabinet

Display cases are made of stainless steel and glass.

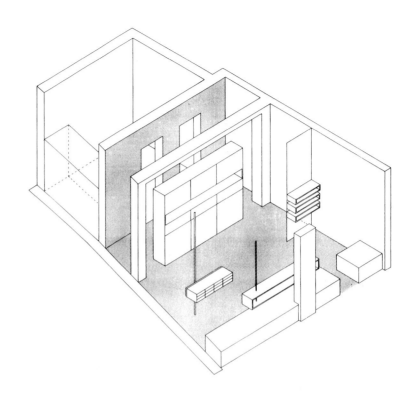

Details of the various display systems.

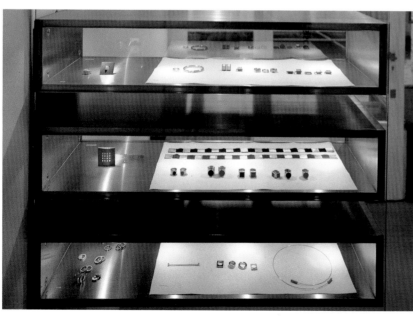

Jigsaw Boutique

The company Jigsaw demonstrated its interest in original design architecture through earlier stores. This project on Bond Street, one of London's most prestigious shopping areas, set out to create a distinctive "spatial logo" suitable for displaying Jigsaw's clothing; an inviting space that would make customers feel comfortable.

The architectural features deliberately minimize the background, shifting the spotlight directly onto the garments.

The façades of the two adjacent buildings combined in this project have undergone various changes over the years. The designers decided to tear down the façades and start from scratch. They created two immense glass fronts with exquisitely finished cement panels. Immediately inside the entry is a magnificently illuminated display area with a 20-ft. ceiling.

The unconventional floor layout was modified to achieve clarity and order. The staircase is the only element that breaks the orthogonal geometry. Visually striking, it indicates the existence of another floor. Four display areas, forming the core of the ground floor, are separated by acrylic screens that provide a feeling of warmth and minimize the structural pillars. The walls are bathed in light, while track lighting focuses on certain areas.

Thanks to the whiteness of the walls and the sublime finish of the granite flooring, the store has a luxurious, sophisticated feel without being opulent. The functional requirements were met by paying careful attention to proportion and by taking advantage of the space's unique expressivity without sacrificing practicality.

Architect:
John Pawson
Collaborator:
Vishwa Kaushal
Photographer:
Richard Glover
Location:
London, UK
Completion date:
1996
Floor space:
6,500 square fe

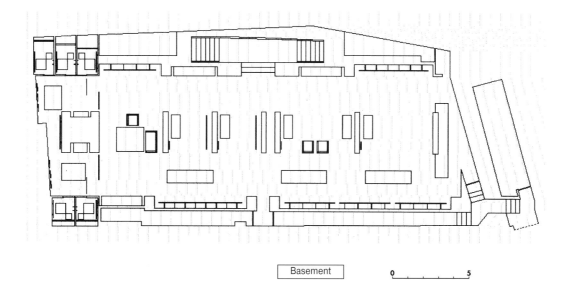

Basement

0 ————— 5

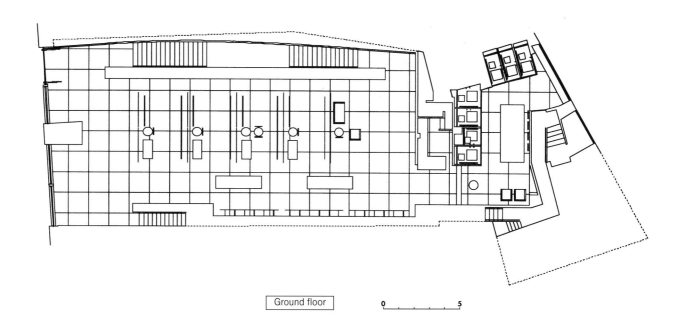

Ground floor

0 ————— 5

Remodeled storefront in glass and black-painted steel.

Detail of the display shelves.

Right. View of the ground floor.

MA Gallery

N

Hiroyuki Arima and his Urban Fourth Studio are beginning to make a name for themselves on the Japanese architectural scene. In a way few others can, they blend traditional sensibility with a progressive, almost futuristic vision of architecture.

Their projects are guided by a respect for materials and by forceful, daring, and exquisite geometric design.

The MA Gallery is in Genkai National Park, a region that lies between sea and mountains, two hours from Fukuoka, Japan. Its five modules atop a steep 55-ft. slope include exhibition space and a workshop for the client, an artist.

Various common materials –cement, cedar planks, corrugated polycarbonate sheets, "tin plate," and wire mesh– were combined to achieve flexible spaces that flow into one another. Another key objective was ensuring that plenty of light filled the exhibition rooms, also used to hold concerts, and the artist's studio, which was designed to be independent, more intimate, and isolated from the rest of the building.

The upper level of the gallery displays works of art and is an ideal place from which to view the Genkai-nada Sea, clearly visible beyond the plain. A glass display case exhibits artwork without blocking the sunlight that filters through to the lower levels and emphasizes the floor-to-floor fluidity.

The rocky surface persuaded the architects to build an independent structure for each floor and module, making it unnecessary to excessively disturb the natural environment. The self-contained structural system means the supports can be in different positions for each floor.

Architects:

Hiroyuki Arima + Urban Fourth

Collaborators:

Sayuri Koda, Toru Sakiyama

Photographer:

Koji Okamoto

Location:

Itoshima-gun, Fukuoka Prefect

Japan

Completion date:

1998

Floor space:

975 square feet

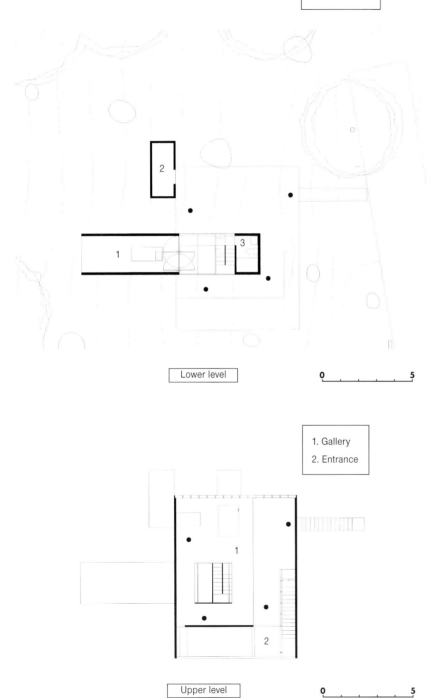

1. Studio
2. Storage
3. Bathroom

Lower level

0   5

1. Gallery
2. Entrance

Upper level

0   5

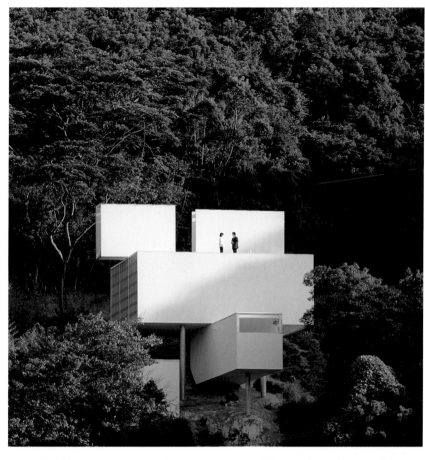

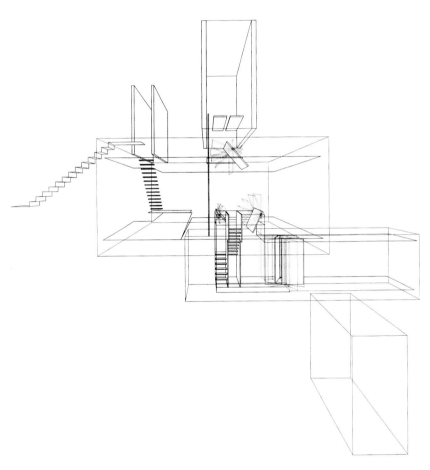

The axonometric view shows the fluidity between spaces.

Dolce & Gabbana Boutique

Dolce & Gabbana's new company image came to fruition in its revamped flagship store in Milan. The distinctive elements of this new image will also reshape their boutiques in London, and in others around the world.

One of the materials used repeatedly in this project is basalt. It covers the entire floor, is used for a plinth along the walls that defines the areas where the clothing and accessories are displayed. Basalt is also gradually transformed into the counter and staircase.

The ceilings have been left plain, free of decoration, except for specially designed light boxes. The fluorescent lights can be directed toward the different display cases. Polycarbonate shades filter the light, softening the effect and bringing warmth to the setting.

Subtle, laminated glass screens with a layer of silk break the pure white of the walls. These partitions conceal the fitting room area, creating an ideal backdrop for the Dolce & Gabbana logo.

Garments are hung from teak racks, either free-standing or attached to the wall. Tables are also made of teak, forming a contrast with the shiny, smooth glass surface of the cabinets. The display furnishings were designed by David Chipperfield and manufactured by B&B Italia.

The architect's austere lines focus attention on the merchandise. To compensate for the minimalist aesthetics, Domenico Dolce and Stefano Gabbana rounded off the boutique's appearance with a range of accessories: baroque chairs, pictures, sculpture, zebra skins, and plants.

Architects:
    David (
P+ARCH
Collaborato
    Filipp
    Ferrar
    Gaspar
Photographe
    Dennis
Location:
    Milan,
Completion
    1999
Floor space
    3,300

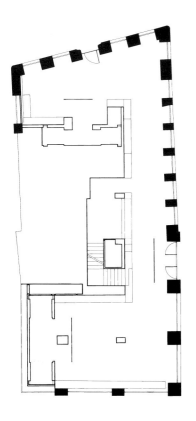

Ground floor

0   5

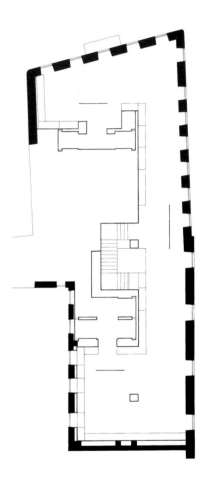

Second floor

0   5

Principe Boutique

As can be seen in other designs of commercial spaces, many boutiques resemble art galleries. This similarity does not come about by chance; it is planned and has a solid basis. These stores do not use normal sales strategies. Instead, the shopper is invited to stroll through an area in which elegance and luxury are expressed in a personal way. Therefore, the handbags and other accessories that are perfectly displayed and illuminated are not there just to be sold. Their presence and arrangement creates an atmosphere, an ambience that is the true value being conveyed. Buying a pair of shoes makes the customer feel as if he or she owns part of this impeccable space.

The relationships among the architecture, the materials used for finishes, lighting, and furniture, and the products themselves are not determined by window dressing or advertising artifice.

The Principe Boutique, in an upscale area of Milan,Italy, is a prime example of how these rules are applied. The limited floor space required the architects to eliminate unnecessary elements and emphasize what remained. Few materials were used. The entire shop is made of glass, steel, wood, and plaster painted white. The floor is marble and the façade contains both clear and translucent glass.

Great care was taken in designing the showcases, which are made of wood, stainless steel, and glass. Individual pieces of furniture provide a flexible display system on three different levels. The technical systems, lighting, and air conditioning are hidden in a false ceiling that opens to illuminate the boutique.

Architects:
Antonio
Collaborato
Patric
Photographe
Gionata
Location:
Milan,
Completion
1998
Floor space
600 sq

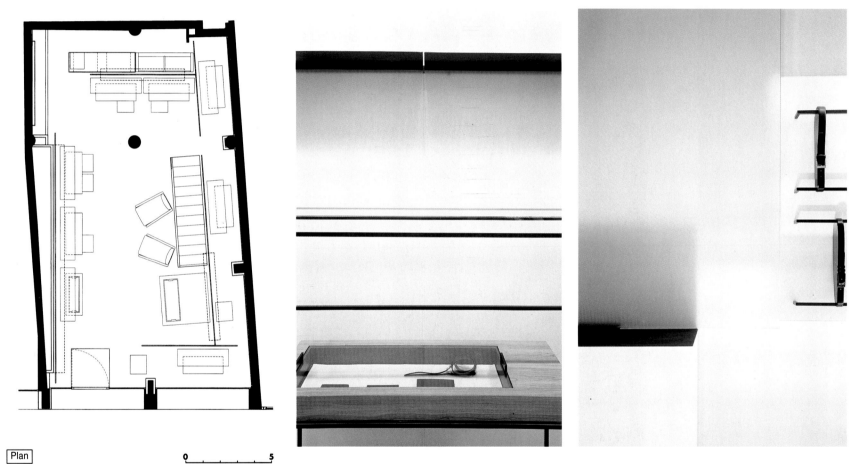

Plan

0 _____ 5

Display systems designed by the architect.

Fausto Santini Boutique

Fausto Santini Boutique in Düsseldorf, Germany, is part of a worldwide project that includes three other shops in Paris, Rome, and Milan. All the stores have achieved a fine balance between the architect's plans and the client's requirements, creating attractive spaces in which to display the products.

The project was dominated by the idea of dehumanizing the spaces, stripping them of dispensable elements and converting them into abstract icons of an exclusively commercial approach that could be implemented anywhere in the world. One key requirement was to make the shop easy to identify with the brand name and the objects on sale.

The concept behind the four boutiques is similar to that of museums. The space is restrained and classic, based on neutrality and rationality, so the items on display play the principal role. The flexibility and, paradoxically, the consistency of the different shops' global image was achieved, in part, by using the same materials and by carefully exploiting each location's potential. All the boutiques are located on the first floor of a typical building in the city's prime shopping area.

Plaster, stone and, above all, wood help create a serene, atmosphere common to all the boutiques. Except for a few concessions to a more modern, abstract style, the mood is reminiscent of the 1930's. The intention was to create a neutral space in which the objects themselves add a dash of color.

Antonio Citterio designed a set of made-to-measure display cases. The most eye-catching is a hollowed-out partition wall. The firm's shoes and bags are presented on limestone slabs, glass shelves with sliding panels, wengué wood panels, and in glass showcases. Most of the displays have their own lighting.

Architects:
    Antonio Citterio and Partners
Collaborator:
    Patricia Viel
Photographer:
    Gionata Xerra
Location:
    Düsseldorf, Germany
Completion date:
    1996
Floor space:
    2,150 square feet

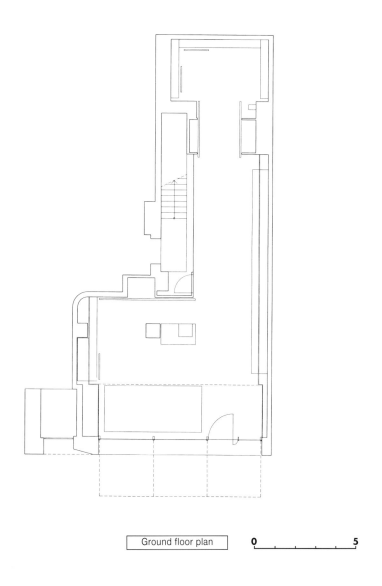

Ground floor plan

0   5

All display systems were designed by Antonio Citterio and Partners.

Louis Vuitton Boutiques

The Louis Vuitton Boutique project in Paris involved a store for the firm's new collection of casual wear, as a complement to the company's classic line of suitcases and accessories.

On a corner along the Champs-Elyseés, in an emblematic 1930's art deco building, the designers created a new bronze and glass façade which seduces the passerby into entering the high rotunda finished in wood and smooth plaster. Numerous paths lead from the entrance, forming multiple routes.
The ambience is devoid of opulence and extravagance.

Peter Marino designed a boutique with clear, sophisticated lines that highlight the items on display.

The street level is visually joined to the basement by a two-story open space of glass decorated with exotic wood inlay. There, another rotunda emphasizes the spatial characteristics of the entrance. The wood floors are covered by rugs and carpets, which add warmth to the showrooms.

There is an alternative entrance to the menswear department. This part of the project received similar treatment: perfectly finished, bright plastering. A bronze staircase and glass elevator connect the two levels.

The London shop is smaller and more restrained, making it easier to identify with minimalist principles. Clothing is exhibited in the niches and on the slender shelves of the partitions.

Again, the materials are smooth plaster and wood, with a staircase and bronze-and-glass elevator.

Except for some strategically placed spotlights, the lighting is hidden behind a false ceiling which does not touch the walls.

Architects:
    Peter Marino & Associates
Photographer:
    David Cardelús
Locations:
    Paris, France
    London, England
Completion date:
    1998
Floor space:
    12,000 square feet (Paris)
    8,000 square feet (London)

Paris boutique: pages 198 to 202.
London boutique: pages 203 to 207.

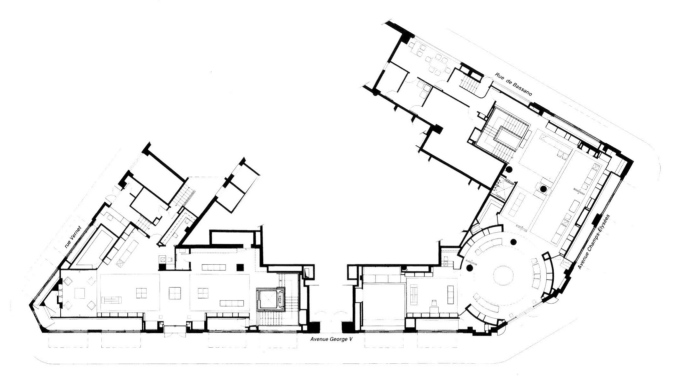

Main floor

0   5

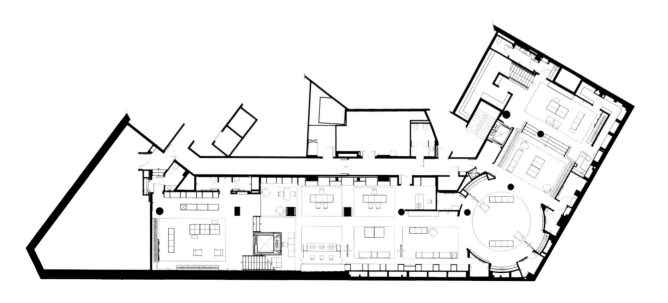

Lower level

0   5

ris boutique is bigger and designed with more sophisticated lines.

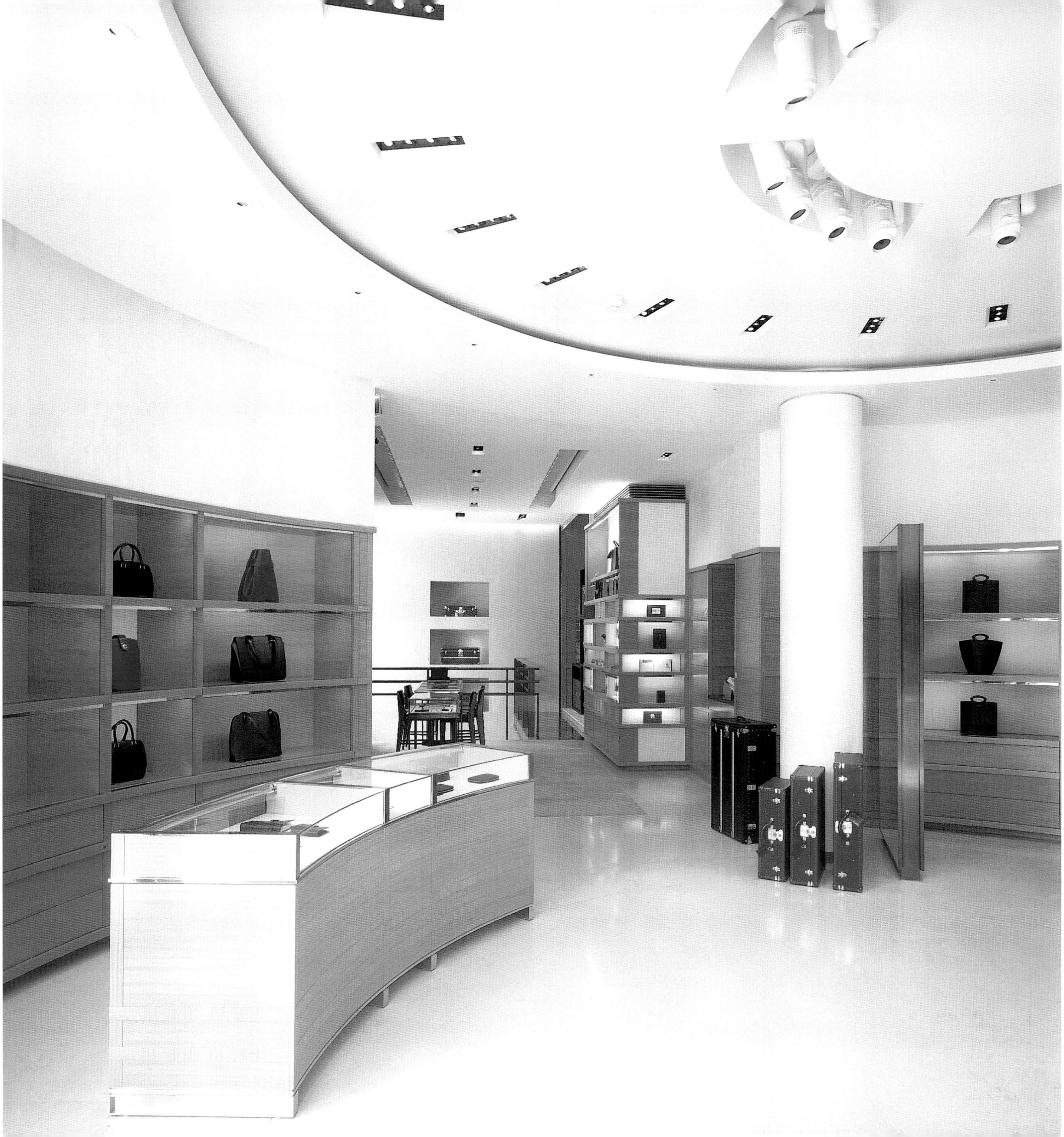

Plans show the complex spaces and paths.

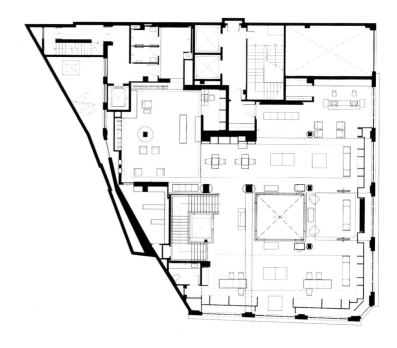

Ground floor 　　　0 ____ 5

Second floor 　　　0 ____ 5

Detail of the façade display cases.

View of the staircase and the elevator.

206

London´s shop is more minimal. The clothes are exhibited in niches and on the shelves of the partitions.

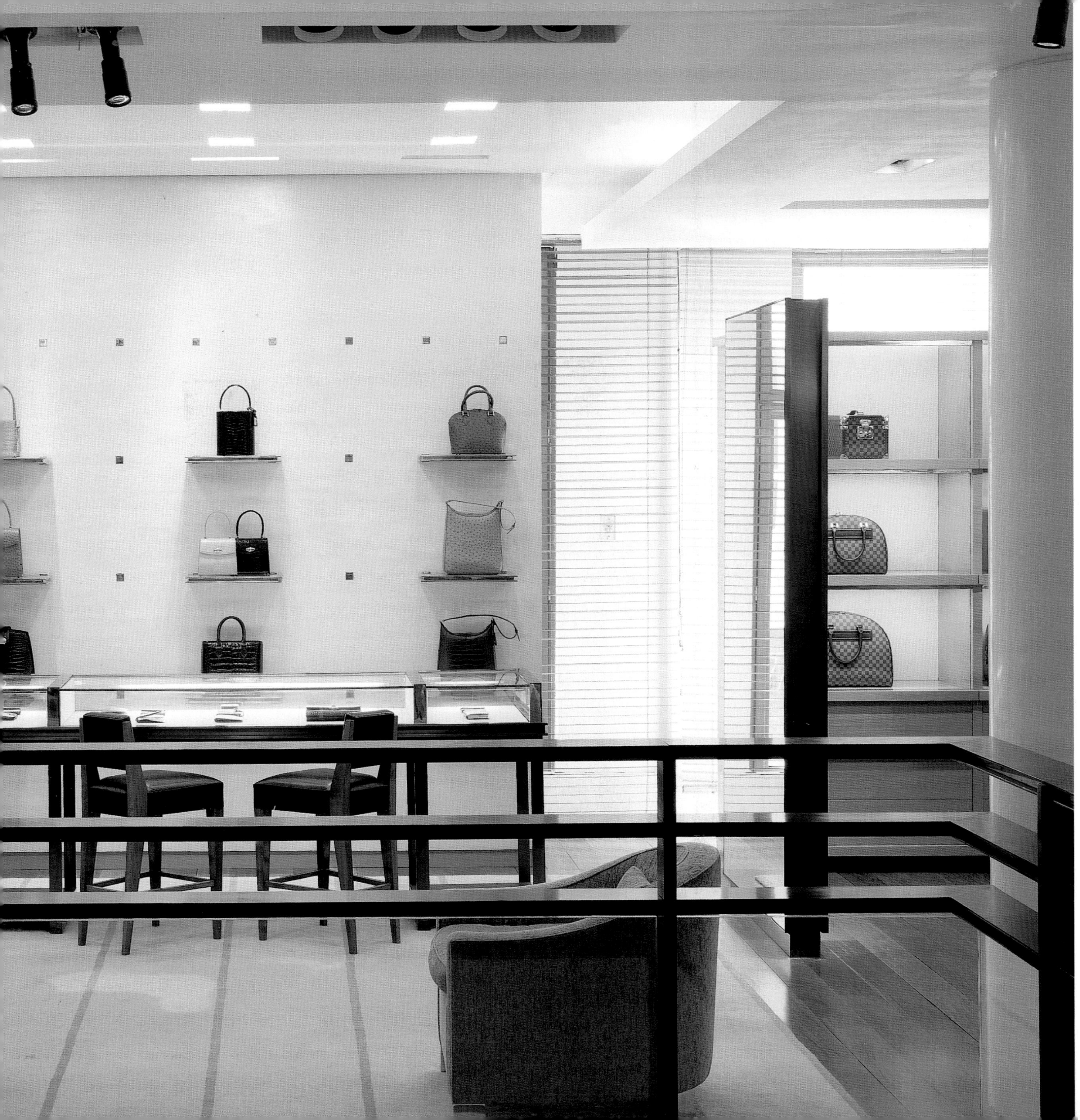